Contemporary
sociology of
the school
General editor
JOHN EGGLESTON

Assessment,
schools and society

CONTEMPORARY SOCIOLOGY
OF THE SCHOOL

PAUL BELLABY
The sociology of comprehensive schooling

PATRICIA BROADFOOT
Assessment, schools and society

BRIAN DAVIES
Social control and education

SARA DELAMONT
Interaction in the classroom

JOHN EGGLESTON
The ecology of the school

ERIC HOYLE
School organization and administration

COLIN LACEY
The socialization of teachers

PETER MUSGRAVE
The moral curriculum: a sociological analysis

ROY NASH
Scholing in rural societies

PHILIP ROBINSON
Education and poverty

MICHAEL STUBBS
Language, schools and classrooms

WILLIAM TYLER
The sociology of educational inequality

TOM WHITESIDE
The sociology of educational innovation

PATRICIA BROADFOOT

Assessment, schools and society

METHUEN

First published in 1979 by Methuen & Co. Ltd
11 New Fetter Lane, London EC4P 4EE
Published in the USA by
Methuen & Co.
in association with Methuen Inc.
733 Third Avenue, New York, NY10017
© 1979 Patricia Broadfoot
Typeset by Inforum Ltd Portsmouth
Printed in Great Britain
by J.W. Arrowsmith Ltd, Bristol

British Library Cataloguing in Publication Data
Broadfoot, Patricia
*Assessment, schools and society. – (Contemporary
sociology of the school).*
1. Students, Rating of
2. Educational sociology
I. Title   II. Series
301.5'6   LB1117
ISBN 0–416–71570–2
ISBN 0–416–71580–X Pbk

CONTENTS

For Mum

Acknowledgements

I wish to take this opportunity of expressing my thanks to all those with whom I have worked during the last few years, to whom I owe a great debt for their contribution to the thinking that has enabled this book to be written. Their names are too numerous to mention — they know who they are.

Specifically I must thank the series editor, John Eggleston, for both his painstaking and constructive comments and his unfailing support. I also wish to thank others who gave of their time and wisdom to comment on early drafts of this book — Margot Cameron-Jones, Bill Cousin, Marjorie Cruickshank, Valerie Dundas-Grant, Colin Lacey.

Finally, I wish to express my gratitude to Mrs Elizabeth Brock for her careful, efficient and at all times speedy, typing.

Editor's introduction

Sociology has changed dramatically in the past decade. Sociologists have provided an ever increasing diversity of empirical and theoretical approaches that are advancing our understanding of the complexities of societies and their educational arrangements. It is now possible to see the over-simplification of the earlier sociological view of the world running smoothly with agreed norms of behaviour, with institutions and individuals performing functions that maintained society and where even conflict was restricted to 'agreed' areas. This normative view of society with its functionalist and conflict theories has now been augmented by a range of interpretative approaches in which the realities of human interaction have been explored by phenomenologists, ethnomethodologists and other reflective theorists. Together they have emphasized the part that individual perceptions play in determining social reality and have challenged many of the characteristics of society that the earlier sociologists had assumed to be 'given'.

The new approaches have had striking effects upon the

sociology of the school. Earlier work was characterized by a range of incompletely examined assumptions about such matters as ability, opportunity and social class. Sociologists asked how working class children could achieve in the schools like middle class children. Now they also ask how a social system defines class, opportunities and achievement. Such concepts and many others such as subjects, the curriculum and even schools themselves are seen to be products of the social system in which they exist. In our study of the school we can now explore more fully the ways in which individual teachers' and students' definitions of their situation help to determine its social arrangements; how perceptions of achievement can not only define achievement but also identify those who achieve; how expectations about schooling can determine the very nature and evaluation of schools.

This series of volumes explores the main areas of the sociology of the school in which new understanding of events is now available. Each introduces the reader to the new interpretations, juxtaposes them against the longer standing perspectives and reappraises the contemporary practice of education and its consequences.

In each, specialist authors develop their own analyses of central issues such as poverty, opportunity, comprehensive schooling, the language and interaction of the classroom, the teachers' role, the ecology of education, and ways in which education acts as an instrument of social control. The broad spectrum of themes and treatments is closely interrelated; it is offered to all who seek new illumination on the practice of education and to those who wish to know how contemporary sociological theory can be applied to educational issues.

A major feature of recent developments in the sociology of the school has been the renewed study of examinations and assessment. For many years we have known that access to and success in examinations has been a key determinant of social mobility. But more recently we have seen more clearly that examinations are important instruments of social control, 'accrediting' individuals and 'legitimating' knowledge. In this volume Patricia Broadfoot draws these sociological analyses together to present a comprehensive account of the consequences of examinations for the life of the classroom. She illuminates her account of events in contemporary Britain with valuable historical and international perspectives.

Yet examinations are now but part of the complex machinery of assessment that links the structure and values of society to the day to day work of the school. Perhaps the most important part of Patricia Broadfoot's volume is her exploration of the new developments in accountability, assessment of performance, monitoring and a range of informal assessment techniques which not only affect classroom life but also adapt and modify the relationship between society and schools.

There is widespread agreement that all who participate in our educational arrangements need to know of the 'micro' and 'macro' consequences of these major changes. Patricia Broadfoot's coherent and original sociological analysis offers us this necessary and timely understanding.

John Eggleston

1

Sociology and assessment

There is a great deal about contemporary educational practice which as a society we tend to take for granted. Often, the more heated the debate about educational issues becomes, the more the real issues are obscured. A notable example of this phenomenon at the time of writing is the concern about supposedly 'falling standards' and the demand for careful monitoring of the work of the nation's schools. The assumptions underlying this public concern are of great interest to the sociologist of education because they reveal the expectations people typically hold of our education system — expectations which are rarely questioned. This book will be concerned with analysing these expectations through a study of the various methods used in schools to assess pupil achievement. The aspects of pupils' performance that schools choose to assess reflect very clearly the functions a particular educational system is required to fulfil. Indeed it could be argued that assessment practices are one of the clearest indices of the relationship between school and society since they provide for communication between the two.

Before starting out on our analysis, however, we must mark out the ground by looking briefly at the nature of educational assessment itself.

The need for assessment

It is very hard to set limits to assessment. Passing judgement is a central part of social behaviour. We are continually passing judgements on our fellows — on their clothes, their accents, their actions, their beliefs — in fact in every area of human life. We pass judgement on products too — on books and television programmes, on buildings and furniture, on art and music, not least on football teams! Since we regulate and give meaning to our own lives by the values we adopt, it is inevitable that our values should influence our interpretation of the actions of others and their results. Most of the time we are probably not aware of the judgements we make for, unlike the drama or music critic whose job it is to evaluate an artistic performance in terms of the prevailing standards of our particular society, very few of us would claim the right to pass a formal judgement in an area in which we have no special expertise. Rather, we appoint and train specialists who become expert at interpreting what they think are the values of society which operate in their own field and we entrust to them the task of being arbiters of the quality of a particular performance. Thus, despite the fact that their criteria are often in fact greatly *avant garde* in comparison with society at large, the decision whether to buy a particular painting for a national collection will be the responsibility of a few individuals whose experience and talent lead the nation to rely on their judgement. Informally of course we still reserve the right for ourselves as individuals to decide what we personally find pleasing or moving, shocking or in bad taste, for such value-judgements are as integral to social life as social life is to being human.

Education is no exception to this general rule. We appoint 'experts' — people with specific qualifications and experience, who are entrusted with making judgements which conform to prevailing social values about desirable achievements. Thus in schools, teachers operate as 'educational critics' and evaluate educational performance in accordance with agreed standards. This evaluation takes many forms: in the classroom it may be the mark given for the weekly test or the ink exercise, or it may be expressed in the end of term class placement, the end of year exam, or the awarding of an external certificate. At the same time evaluation is continually taking place as part of the interaction between teacher and pupil: 'Johnny is always gazing out of the window', 'Susan will need more help with her handwriting', 'Lorraine always looks so untidy'. The same informal judgements are likewise continually being made by the pupils about the teacher and about each other: 'Mrs Brown is even more boring today than usual', 'Sir had no right to tell Tom off like that', 'Tony is a creep'. Such evaluation, overt and covert, formal and informal, familiar to all of us, is as integral to school life as it is to all human relationships, immensely powerful but seldom acknowledged.

Our first task is to consider why such judgements in the school context are of interest to the sociologist of education. In order to do this we must temporarily forgo a consideration of specifically school practices and address the question of assessment at its most general level — the kinds of decision every society must make about assessing the performance of its potential entrants. Put simply, these decisions concern: Who to assess? What to assess? When to assess? How to assess and why assess? The answers made to these questions will reflect closely the social reality of a particular society.

Education as socialization

Education is a major instrument of socialization. In simple societies it may be almost exclusively what we may call 'primary' socialization — the training of children in the appropriate forms of behaviour and skills required by all members of that society. Secondary socialization — the preparation of children for particular roles in society — will be largely restricted to those societies whose complexity allows their members to pursue a much greater variety of interests and to specialize in the development of specific talents. Such complex societies in particular require individuals to undertake a great variety of occu-

13

pations to maintain the division of labour which characterizes them. It is in these latter societies, therefore, that formal provision for secondary socialization is made in the institution of an education system, which prepares youngsters for a variety of future roles. However, whether education consists simply of the passing on of a unified body of skills necessary for survival, often by elder siblings or, at the other end of the scale, is transmitted through the highly bureaucratized, elaborate and costly system which complex industrialized societies have typically evolved to provide for the wide range of specialist skills they require, some kind of assessment procedure will be necessary. Not least because the willingness of the individual to submit to assessment reflects and reinforces his commitment to joining that particular society. Thus in simple societies the prevalance of *rites de passage*, often coinciding with puberty — the time at which a child is able and expected to take on the full obligations of an adult member of society — reflect the kinds of formal assessment procedures instituted in such societies. These are essentially 'qualifying' tests, the time at which a youngster can demonstrate his mastery of the norms and skills necessary for effective participation in that society, thereby allowing the existing members of that society to judge his fitness to belong to it. In such a situation the assessment procedures will be largely undifferentiated, except perhaps between boys and girls, since this is the only significant division of labour. Thus the questions posed above of who to assess, what to assess, when, how and why, will be equally unproblematic. All aspirant members (who) — and this will be almost exclusively children, since it is rare for adults to move from society to society in such situations — will be adjudged at the same stage of their life (when), on the same relevant criteria of basic competence in necessary skills (what), in order to ensure the continued survival of the society (why). The remaining question — how — will be largely determined by the need for validity in the test, that is, that the skills assessed match as closely as possible the potential real life requirements. Thus the Red Indian boy was traditionally required to slay his own buffalo and demonstrate his ability to provide all the essentials of life for himself from its carcass. Masai youngsters are required to demonstrate their ability to survive alone and unprovisioned in the bush for a substantial period of time. In many societies boys must demonstrate their ability to be the courageous warriors needed to defend their society by submitting bravely to the pain of circumcision. It is important to note, however, that in such simple societies it is expected that *all* members should pass the test: the emphasis is on qualifying, not selection.

I have digressed at some length from the contemporary school situation in order to clarify by the most simple examples the relationship between educational assessment and society. That the *rites de passage* of our own society are highly complex and problematic, differentiated and continually changing, is a direct reflection of the similar nature of the mechanisms of secondary socialization which provide for the division of labour characterizing our society. We now turn, therefore, to a consideration of the much more complex issues involved in the decisions to be made about assessment practices in advanced industrial societies.

Who to assess?

Anyone taking part in the formal education system is a candidate for assessment. Normally this will be children since they are compelled to be at school for some eleven years. It is increasingly common, however, for adults to re-submit themselves for assessment as the requirements of rapid social and technological change make re-training for different occupations more and more necessary. Much more problematic is the issue of whether to assess all school pupils at the same age, in the same way. Until very recently, for example, some, and even a majority of pupils in most countries of Western Europe have been denied the opportunity even to compete with their more academic peers for many external certificates. The rationale for this significant departure from the practice of simple societies is a very relevant sociological question, as indeed are the effects of such a situation on the pupils in school. This will become apparent in our discussion of the historical and contemporary trends in assessment practice in chapters 2 and 3.

What to assess?

This is a much more complex issue than the previous question because the content of assessment is of interest both as it concerns a commodity — certain types of achievement — that some may be better able to come by than others, and substantively as a reflection of the particular skills and knowledge valued in the education system. Since in many ways education can be seen as the apprenticeship for membership of a particular society and, in complex societies, membership of a particular *level* of society, the achievement recognized for reward in the education system will tend to dominate what is taught. The power of 'the assessment tail to wag the curriculum dog' and to impede curriculum development despite a not insubstantial body of educational opinion in favour of change in curriculum content and more flexible, progressive child-centred teaching methods, is reflected in the very slow development of such innovations in the secondary school in comparison with the primary school, now freed from formal assessment.

In simple societies, as we have seen, there is likely to be little discussion about the desirable content of 'education' and little need to discriminate between the members of society in terms of their mastery of it. In the stratified societies of industralized nations, some sociologists (such as Bourdieu, 1974) have argued that the necessity for distinguishing between individuals and the high stakes involved results in powerful groups imposing what may seem quite arbitrary criteria for such ratings but which in fact reflect the characteristics on which that power is based and constitute a considerable handicap to the success of children from other social groups in the educational system. These criteria are normally based on certain academic and particularly linguistic achievements although informally they may often include speech, dress and other social behaviour as well. The choice of academic ability alone for formal assessment and certification rather than, for example, non-cognitive social skills such as co-operation and reliability, leadership and perseverance, parental and citizenship skills — all ostensibly more relevant to the majority of prospective members of society and to employers than academic skills — closely reflects the relationship between school and society. We shall consider the cause and effects of this focus on academic ability in chapter 4.

When to assess?

There must be assessment when there are decisions to be made about alternative routes in the educational system. These decisions may be voluntary and based on informal discussion between teacher, parent and pupil, or they may be imposed through a 'weeding out' procedure. Thus for example the 11+ selection in Britain has been largely abandoned since the formal necessity for the allocation of pupils to different types of secondary school and thus to different educational routes has ceased with the institution of the comprehensive school. Informal assessments, however, in the form of school records, may still follow the child from primary to secondary school where they may well be used for internal, informal 'tracking' in the receiving school.

It may be argued that in some ways the question of 'when to assess' is meaningless since, as we have seen, informal assessment at classroom level is an inevitable and continual process. The question is significant though with regard to formal assessment since the decision to have certification at what is now the end of compulsory schooling, yet which was, when certification was instituted, undertaken a considerable time *after* the statutory school-leaving age, has profound implications for the changing nature of the educational system and the pupils within it, as we shall see in chapter 3.

How to assess?

The significance of this question lies not so much in the particular ways found to answer it but in the dominance of the question itself over the other questions concerning assessment in contemporary debates. Even a cursory glance at the literature on assessment reveals the predominance of concern about techniques— the accuracy of formal examinations, the advantages and disadvantages of objective tests, the potential of item-banking, the relative merits of various moderation and scaling techni-

17

ques, the sophisticated statistical procedures being developed for fixing discrimination and facility values, the debate over the desirability of continuous versus point in time assessment — to name but a few. The debate — and there is currently a good deal of it — is conducted almost entirely in this arena, the arena of efficiency. The heated discussion initiated in England in this decade by the Schools Councils proposals for what were, in reality, fairly minor changes in the structure of certification awards at 16, 17 and 18+ was matched by a similar debate in Scotland following on the publication of a Report there in 1977 of a Secretary of State's Committee on Assessment and Certification. The focus of such discussion is overwhelmingly on examining current practice and working out how it may be changed to become more efficient and thus ostensibly more just. This emphasis on short-term, pragmatic issues, this location of the problematic essentially within the *status quo*, is highly significant because of the legitimating influence of assessment procedures in reinforcing a particular understanding of the desirable nature of education. To put it another way, if only the efficiency of assessment practices is questioned and not their purposes and effects, and if, as I have argued, formal assessment procedures exert a strong influence on the curriculum in reinforcing a particular interpretation of the nature of education — in our society one based on achievement stratified according to academic ability — then the scope for educational change and reform is very limited.

The seriousness of this issue of how to assess is compounded by the effects of the use of particular assessment techniques. We may consider, for example, how the use of extended essay-type questions in examinations and continuous assessment perhaps favour pupils with certain kinds of class-based linguistic competence (Bernstein, 1971). The predominance of norm-referenced assessment which ranks pupils according to their relative achievement as opposed to criterion-referenced assessment of the driving-test type which simply records pupils' attainment of specific curricular goals individually, reflects and compounds the competitiveness which is a characteristic feature of our society. Even the very assumption that educational attainment can be measured by any external means rather than by the pupil

18

himself is an important influence on the organization of education and reflects the very deep-rooted social forces underlying the education system. We have only to look at the relatively recent institution of formal educational assessment— in universities, for example, not until the late nineteenth century — to realize that such assessment is by no means an inevitable aspect of education.

We shall consider these issues in detail in the substantive analyses of later chapters. My intention at this stage is to look at the contribution the sociologist can make in redressing the emphases of the professional test constructor and in extending the debate beyond the pragmatic to reveal the causes and effects on the educational process of some normally unquestioned assumptions.

Why assess?

I have left the most profound question about educational assessment till last since in many ways it subsumes the others and thus merits a more detailed discussion. In seeking to conceptualize the issues involved in this question I have attempted an overview of the principal uses of school assessment and by so doing aim to clarify the scope for, and importance of, the sociological study of these practices which will be our concern in the ensuing chapters of this book. It is already apparent that assessment can take many different forms. We shall look first at the more obvious, formal functions of assessment since these conform most readily to our common-sense understanding of the nature of educational assessment and figure most prominently in public debate. These overt purposes of formal assessment can be divided into two reasonably distinct areas — accountability and certification — and we shall deal with them separately.

Accountability The education system is an extremely costly enterprise and so, not unreasonably, it has to account for itself to the society which pays for it. Not only do schools have to account to their local authority for the way money is spent, they have to 'produce the goods' in educational terms. In the nineteenth century this need for accountability was expressed in the 'payment by results' system in which schools were given money in return for bringing individual pupils up to the required standard in certain specified areas. The deleterious effects of this system, resulting as it did in cramming and coercion and almost no scope for response by the teacher to the needs of the individual child, are fortunately a thing of the past. However, the contemporary presence of a large army of local and national school inspectors testifies to the continuing concern that schools should be accountable to society for the investment in them as measured by the achievements of their pupils and their conformity to accepted practice. We do not have to look further than the William Tyndale affair (see for example Gretton and Jackson, 1976) or the sacking of certain radical headmasters in recent years to see the sanctions which come into operation when individual head teachers or groups of staff attempt to depart from the accepted norms of school conduct. Indeed it is not hard to discern in England an increasing concern for accountability in recent years and a consequent pressure towards a more precise monitoring of educational standards. Bourdieu and Passeron (1977) have suggested that the extension of academic education to a new population not equipped with suitable skills to benefit from it is likely to result in a lowering of academic standards and public concern. Certainly in England there is an obvious connection between comprehensivization and the consequent increased visibility of the failures of the erstwhile secondary modern pupil, and between raising the school leaving age, opening up public examinations to a much greater number of pupils, and the growing concern with falling standards. Although the evidence points to more pupils both attempting and gaining external qualifications, the insecurity induced by such major organizational and curricular changes has led to the institution of new 'quality control' mechanisms and in particular, the D.E.S. Assessment of Performance Unit which has found favour in many parts of the world (Marjoram, 1977). This Unit is not concerned with identifying the performance of individual pupils but is designed to assess the overall standards being achieved at the various stages of schooling and in different aspects of the curriculum.

Such sampling of achievement, it is felt, will allow policy-makers to chart the return on investment being achieved within the educational system as a whole.

This accountability aspect of educational assessment is very significant in its impact on the nature of schooling since it reflects and reinforces the legitimacy of existing educational practice and effectively prevents any very significant departures from the *status quo*. It is thus equally significant for our study of the relationship between schooling and society for it reveals very clearly the expectations the education system is intended to fulfil in our society and the constraints operating to prevent changes in the system. In consequence, the scope of education to be an instrument of social change is equally curtailed.

Certification   Certification is perhaps the most commonly recognized function of school assessment. At the end of his school career, or a major stage of it, a pupil has the opportunity to demonstrate his achievements in relation to the goals of the educational system. His performance in apparently fair and objective tests is formally evaluated by 'experts', usually teachers, appointed for their knowledge both of the subject-matter and of appropriate standards. The results of this evaluation are compared with those of a large number of other pupils, thereby providing another means of 'quality control' on the system. This is not the specific intention of the exercise, however. The major aim is to rank the pupil in comparison with his fellow competitors against pre-determined criteria, a ranking which has a close relationship with entry to various points in the occupational hierarchy, allowing further and higher educational instructors and employers to select those whom they consider have 'performed' sufficiently well and have therefore obtained the requisite necessary entrance qualifications. The extreme importance of certification as an influence both on educational practice and the wider society emerges from this 'gate-keeper' role, by which it can open and close doors for individuals to future life chances. The certification process is indeed the epitome of the overtly meritocratic basis of our society, since in theory it allows free competition based on academic ability and industry and thus is regarded as the fairest basis for the alloca-

21

tion of opportunities for high status or remunerative careers. The discovery that the process is not in fact 'fair' and in particular favours pupils with certain kinds of home background, was a major achievement of sociologists of education in the fifties and sixties for whom the relationship between social class background and school achievement was a major preoccupation for many years.

The fact that the assessments are at best only a rough estimate of particular kinds of ability despite the statistical finesse of the processing of the results and the large body of research directed towards improving their accuracy, has been extensively documented in a large number of research studies since the seminal work of Hartog and Rhodes in 1935. The vagaries of pupil performance and especially of exam stress, of differences between markers and the difficulty of questions, are only some of the more significant causes of inaccuracy which would seem to be largely unavoidable. It may well be partly for this reason that such certificate results are a very weak guide to the likely quality of future job or higher education performance. Indeed Powell (1973) has documented a whole series of other influences on attainment in higher education of which the most obvious are motivation and effort, but which also include quite subtle dimensions excluded from certification assessment, such as intraversion and extraversion and confidence.

I will not dwell further at this stage of a brief overview of assessment practices on this particular issue, since our concern must be principally to examine the *reasons* for the adoption of particular assessment practices and the effect of such decisions on education and society. Thus we should be interested to know why it is that, despite its palpably poor predictive power, certification is so widely used for occupational selection. The answers to this question will be of central importance to the analysis.

Motivation Turning now to the informal functions of assessment, we must consider that argument which holds sway with teachers, parents and pupils alike — that assessment is an important source of motivation. The 'carrot and stick' principle has wide currency. The reward for good performance and the punishment for an inadequate effort is a reality we all have

22

known only too well as the silence ticks away in the examination hall. Any proposal to abandon competitive assessment meets with an outcry among teachers who fear the removal of one of the most powerful weapons in their armoury. Indeed, the 'bait' is so powerful that some research of my own revealed a majority of twelve-year old pupils who, when asked why they thought they were studying a particular subject, replied that it was to get their 'O' levels — they had been well indoctrinated (Broadfoot, 1977) ! The converse of this situation is, of course, also true — the increasing lack of motivation among those pupils who are not taking external examinations, whose assessments are rarely positive enough to motivate them to try harder, and for whom no very tempting bait can be offered in an educational system that recognizes in its assessment procedures only one kind of ability — the kind which, by definition, they do not have.

This motivational aspect of assessment is important too as an agent of social control. Motivation is dependent on valued rewards and rewards are dependent on appropriate performance. Whatever educational behaviour or achievement is ultimately rewarded in society with the sought after occupational roles, will be the behaviour and achievements towards which aspirants are motivated. The teacher of a non-examined subject knows this only too well. In our society, for various historical and economic reasons which will become apparent, we choose to assess mainly academic ability. We do not choose, by and large, to assess in any formal way non-cognitive qualities such as effort, co-operation, leadership, responsibility or useful experience in extra-curricular activities such as school plays, social service units, outdoor pursuits or debating societies, although of course information on such activities is often supplied in confidential references. Since assessment in such activities and abilities is not part of the formal assessment system, the influence of which permeates right through the informal assessment network, these activities do not provide an alternative source of motivation or self-valuation for pupils. In consequence a potential source of motivation for non-academic pupils and a potential mechanism for the development of many personal qualities which most of us would regard as desirable for future members of society, are neglected. Finally we must turn to the remaining function of assessment which we will call 'diagnosis'.

Diagnosis To examine diagnostic assessment we must come down to the level of the individual classroom, its day-to-day teaching and learning and the evaluation of that learning. We have seen that passing judgements on each other in any form of interaction is inevitable and often quite unconscious. No doubt teachers are constantly assessing pupils on all sorts of criteria not relevant to the educational enterprise at all. In particular they will be constantly judging the behaviour of their pupils, looking for the signs of trouble which may necessitate a change in their own behaviour in order to maintain the control they regard as a necessary precondition of teaching and learning. They will, however, be making more conscious diagnostic evaluation of the learning process itself, trying to gauge the progress and problems of individual pupils in order that they may provide appropriate help and encouragement. Teachers need, too, to evaluate their own teaching in order to judge the value of particular teaching strategies and to discover to what extent the class as a whole has mastered a particular unit of work and thus can usefully be moved on to the next topic. Teachers have many techniques available to enable them to make such judgements. Research shows, for example (Brown and McIntyre, 1977), that on average, teachers may spend almost half their time on oral questioning, partly of course as a teaching tool to move the lesson on, but mainly to assess the understanding of individual pupils and, in aggregate, the class as a whole. In addition, marking written work, chatting to pupils, and even facial expressions will reveal relevant diagnostic information. To the extent that the teacher is relating to the needs and interests of the individual pupil, this purpose of assessment would seem to approximate perhaps most closely to a child-centred interpretation of education. Indeed, the correspondence between the greatly increased emphasis on 'progressive' child-centred teaching methods and the decline of formal assessment in the primary school, seems to support the view that assessment can be divorced from social selection requirements and be geared only to the learning of the individual child. Appearances are deceptive, however, for during the ongoing interaction between teacher and pupil, and even between the pupils themselves, over the weeks and months pupils come to an often unconscious assessment of themselves and their performance in relation to each other as they strive to achieve the socially-defined goals which underlie the teacher's activities. Although the teacher may seek to respond to the variety of pupil needs and interests, pupils become labelled by the teacher in relation to various pre-existing stereotypes of 'the good pupil', 'lazy', 'dull', 'bright' and so on, as we shall see when we examine this process in more detail in chapter 5. Gradually, pupils too come to recognize that only particular kinds of achievement are valued and they learn to assess themselves and adjust their expectations accordingly. The internalization by pupils of such assessments results in time in the very clear differences of behaviour and motivation characterizing those labelled 'bright' and marked out for success and those 'less able' pupils destined for failure.

The way forward

In this chapter I have sought to establish what we mean by assessment and to raise some of the more important sociological questions it implies. The remainder of the book will be concerned with applying these questions to the origins, growth and possible future developments in the assessment practices typically found in industrial societies and by so doing, to provide insights not only into the functions of assessment, but into the nature of industrial mass society itself. In particular such an analysis must reveal the dilemma which has inevitably characterized the development of public education systems in industrial society — namely the conflict between education as a means of liberation and education as a means of social control (Katz, 1965).

Without exception, formal education systems as we know them developed in societies in which traditional inequalities of wealth and power were rapidly being transformed and reinforced in order to provide for that hierarchical division of labour necessary for mass production. As we shall see in chapter 2, these education systems developed both as a means of providing a labour force equipped with the new knowledge and skills required (Coleman, 1968) and as a means of regulating social mobility in the face of the breakdown of more traditional forms of control. Thus it was that assessment procedures developed as the main mechanism both of providing for such regulation and of attesting to the possession of the required knowledge and skills. An analysis of developments in educational assessment procedures reveals more clearly than that of perhaps any other aspect of the education system, the irreconcilable demands which must be put on education in a stratified society. On the one hand it is possible to see the institution of various kinds of educational assessment as crucial steps in the fight against nepotism and inefficiency and in opening up opportunity for social mobility to a quite unprecedented extent. On the other hand it is important to recognize the role of assessment in limiting such mobility and even more crucially, in legitimating what is essentially still an education system strongly biased in favour of traditional privilege. If this latter aspect of educational assessment dominates the analyses offered in this book, it is justified by the need to redress the balance in thinking about assessment, which hitherto has been almost totally dominated by a liberal and pragmatic perspective.

It is necessary to point out, however, that the contradiction I have identified goes beyond any simple conspiracy theory or political argument. As is evident from contemporary trends towards selection and elitism even in people's democracies such as the USSR and China (Bonavia, 1978), the contradiction is, in many ways, an economic one, between the need to produce as quickly and efficiently as possible those who will lead society in the national and international economic battle, as against the commitment typically found in both liberal democracies and socialist States to creating equal opportunity for growth and development among the mass of the population. Thus, given the apparent inevitability of an elite in the hierarchical structure of industrial society, it is important to recognize this dual role of educational assessment in allowing both the identification and, significantly, the perpetuation of this elite. But set against this must be the recognition that educational assessment has been highly instrumental too in creating more open and fair access to that elite.

Thus the approach of this book is essentially eclectic, drawing, perhaps unforgivably in the eyes of some sociologists, on a variety of perspectives on the nature of society for its analyses. Recognizing the dilemma set out above, the book can offer no ready solutions, even at a theoretical level, to the problems identified. But the first step towards any solution, if it exists, must be an analysis of the problem — an analysis which, in relation to educational assessment, has been almost totally lacking up to now. This omission itself must have a profound influence on educational policy and practice (Bacharach and Baratz, 1962). The transition from the identification of a problem to suggestions for its solution necessarily involves value-judgements. In chapter 6 I take what, given a commitment to mass education (not necessarily the same as mass schooling), must be the logical position in the light of the liberation-control dilemma in which educational assessment is embroiled, in suggesting that the second step towards a solution, after the first step of analysis, must be an increasing emphasis on those aspects of assessment integral to personal development and learning. Implicit in this position too is a commitment to seeking to divorce learning for as long as possible from the damaging effects of assessment as an instrument of selection and control. It must, however, become increasingly apparent in the analysis, how closely intertwined the education system and assessment practices have become since their shared origins in the mid-nineteenth century. Like the honeysuckle and the bindweed, they may now be so inseparable that any attempt to release the education system from the constrictions of assessment procedures would result in the collapse of the system itself. It will be possible to trace from the most micro level of classroom interaction and the class test through to the more macro manifestations of assessment in the certificate examination and national monitoring procedures, a single underlying rationale which embodies the contradictory purposes of the system and powerfully controls the nature of its goals and rewards. The exploration of this relationship and its effects will be our primary goal.

2

An historical perspective: the origins of formal assessment in England and Wales

It seems scarcely credible in our qualification-dominated society that formal educational assessment — particularly as we have come to know it in the guise of public examinations — is only a little over a century old. It is now as difficult for us to imagine schooling without examinations as it is to imagine society without the State-provided, compulsory, mass education they heralded. It would have been equally difficult for pre-nineteenth-century society to have envisaged these developments, for apart from isolated historical examples — such as the civil service entrance examinations instituted in imperial China — the notion of *educational* qualifications as such finds its roots in the combined growth of political democracy and the industrial capitalism of the nineteenth century. This being so, one could easily trace very similar developments in educational assessment from these nineteenth-century origins in any industrializing country, but for the sake of simplicity we shall confine our account to the essentially typical case-study of such developments in England and Wales. In this chapter we shall consider the economic and social forces that led to the initial institution of various types of 'quality-control' mechanisms in education and to the massive development of educational assessment over the last hundred years or so. We shall examine why it was that formal academic testing in particular became so quickly institutionalized in the emergent national educational system and ere long became invested with a legitimacy as unassailable as the headmaster's gown (Bell and Grant, 1974).

Pre-nineteenth-century England was an essentially static society in which social, occupational and personal roles were bound up together and determined very largely by birth. For most people schooling was irrelevant to the process of occupational selection but rather was important in providing (for those who had any at all) differential socialization experiences which served as a preparation for the very different future life-styles of the various social strata. Assessment, if it existed at all, was as a result, essentially also a formality. Writing in 1778, Vicessimus Knox provides a graphic testimony to the mainly social nature of education at this time and the consequent insignificance of formal assessment, in his disgusted description of finals examinations at Oxford University. 'As neither the officer, nor anyone else, usually enters the room (for it is considered very ungenteel), the examiners (usually three M.A.'s of the candidate's own choice) and the candidates often converse on the last drinking bout or on horses, or read the newspaper, or a novel, or divert themselves as well as they can in any manner until the clock strikes eleven, when all parties descend and the "testimonium" is signed by the masters' (quoted by Lawson and Silver, 1973). In effect, four years' residence was the only qualification for a degree — not an inappropriate training for an elite for which the qualifications were almost entirely social.

Soon after the beginning of the nineteenth century, this essentially static picture began to change. Whether you attribute this change to 'political radicalism joined with the Evangelical Revival and the stirrings of Benthamite reform' (Maclure, 1965), expressed in a rising moral and political concern amongst philanthropists at this time for social order and justice, or by contrast, to a concern to find a means of stemming the lawlessness and debauchery which had become characteristic of the new industrial cities (Johnson, 1976; Barnard, 1961), both explanations testify to the new demands the burgeoning industrial capitalist economy was making on educational provision. These demands too were very soon reflected in the development of assessment procedures as tools by which schooling might be made responsive to the needs of the economy. It is possible to identify four interrelated but nevertheless distinct themes in the development of assessment practices at this time, which reflect clearly the changes that were taking place in the social role of education and indeed the issues that have come to dominate education in modern industrial societies ever since. For convenience, we shall call them 'competence'; 'content', 'competition' and 'control'.

Competence

The men who led the industrial revolution and the economic expansion of Victorian England were utilitarian, pragmatic and essentially rational men who put their faith in science and individual responsibility. Thus it was that many of the more cohesive professions began to feel the need to rationalize their organization and to define a specific level of competence for which visible testimony could be produced. Living in a free market economy, they were not slow to recognize the value that would accrue to individual practitioners through the creation of a monopoly over a particular profession, the entry to which was controlled according to fairly rigid standards of professional competence. Thus it was that in 1815 the first professional qualifying examinations were instituted by the Society of Apothecaries to ensure that doctors were adequately trained. The institution of written examinations for solicitors followed in 1835 and for accountants in 1880. Gradually, 'the lazy doctrine that men are much of a muchness gave way to a higher respect for merit and for more effectual standards of competence' (Morley's *Life of Gladstone*, quoted in the Beloe Report).

However the innovation of such qualifying examinations had several more general and unlooked for influences on education. Firstly, since these examinations were associated with high-status professions, the model of the written, theoretical test they used became invested with a similar high status — a status it still retains. Secondly, as Dore (1976) argues, the institution of formal examinations was made possible by, and was a symptom of, a more profound change — the systematization of the body of principles on which the work of the profession was based and its rationalization into a form which made it at least partly susceptible to teaching and learning in the classroom, thereby greatly enhancing the importance of schooling. The third outcome of the innovation of professional examinations was the impact it had on vocational training and qualifications in other types of occupation. Although 'on the job' apprenticeship training, traditional to many occupations, still persists even in those professions which early instituted examinations, the ending of the almost feudal 'whole man' concept of apprenticeship (Montgomery, 1965) was not slow to follow the increasing emphasis on *educational* qualifications and the change to contractual, and impersonal employment. Recent studies of apprenticeship (for example Ryrie and Weir, 1978) confirm this trend away from 'on the job' training in favour of the acquisition of more adaptable qualifications in educational institutions of various kinds.

Finally and most fundamentally, the institution of examinations related quite specifically to a particular vocation, marked the beginning of a trend away from the taking of ascribed occupational roles based on hereditary wealth and breeding alone — or lack of it — to a situation in which such roles were ostensibly at least the result of individual achievement and merit. It is possible to argue that this move away from the simple ascription of occupational roles was indeed the inevitable result of the earlier major social upheavals in religion, knowledge and politics which found expression in the Reformation, the Enlightenment and the French Revolution, for in these three movements can be traced new rational, egalitarian and individualistic ideologies which, incubated in the industrial revolution, soon found their expression in the explosion of practices requiring formal demonstrations of competence. The notion of individual responsibility which Weber showed so clearly to be one of the most important contributions of Protestantism to the development of capitalism, was as clearly the *contribution of capitalism* to the developing educational system in the form of *individualistic* assessment. Although it was to be a long time before ascription, patronage and nepotism died out — if indeed they have — the fact that a variety of important social positions could no longer be procured without *at least* demonstrated competence, was highly instrumental in the birth of the meritocratic ethos which has characterized not only England, but to a greater or lesser extent all Western industrial societies since that time.

Content

Universities could not be long in following the example set by the professions in instituting formal entrance examinations, nor could the schools resist the backwash effect. The mid-nineteenth century saw a gradual change not only in the mechanisms of assessment, but in the content of schooling itself as it reflected changing educational aims.

In the elite public schools the emphasis on toughness, team-spirit and leadership continued to dominate for those future leaders of the Empire, Parliament and the Army whose elite status was so firmly ascribed that they could continue for a time to hold themselves aloof from the growing competition for educational qualifications. In the flourishing grammar schools in which were to be found the aspirants to the newly-created clerical, scientific and managerial jobs, there was little leisure or need for such character development and, instead, these schools were increasingly oriented to the burgeoning industry of competitive examinations. The rapid growth of examinations at this time may be indicated by the massive increase in the numbers of those taking the Department of Science and Art examinations which grew from a modest 5,466 in 1865 to 202,868 in 1895 and included as many candidates from mechanics' institutes and other similar institutions as it did from school. Indeed, many Victorians saw success in examinations as a guarantee not only of knowledge, but also of those qualities so necessary in middle-rank occupations — common sense and diligence (Roach, 1971).

But, very quickly after the institution of university-regulated school examinations in the 1850s, the development of 18+ and girls' examinations by Cambridge University in 1869 and the

City and Guild's examinations in practical subjects in 1880, a practice which had initially been adopted as essentially a means of quality control began to exercise an undesirable effect on the curriculum. Edmond Holmes' famous work *What is and what might be*, published in 1911, expresses a view of the undesirable effects of examinations increasingly recognized by people at this time. 'A school that is ridden by the examination incubus is charged with deceit . . . all who become acclimatised to the influence of the system — pupils, teachers, examiners, employers of labour, parents, M.P.s and the rest, fall victims and are content to cheat themselves with outward and visible signs — class lists, orders of merit — as being of quasi-divine authority.'

Concern about the effects this proliferation of examinations was having even at the higher elementary school level led the Board of Education, which had been set up in 1899 and included among its functions the running of non-elementary schools, to publish a report of its Consultative Committee in 1911 which urged instead of examinations for school-leavers the use of a more appropriate school record and a closer liaison with employers. This attempt to encourage a more relevant and vocational emphasis in assessment was as unsuccessful as the subsequent Government Circular of 1913 which sought to encourage a more vocationally-oriented curriculum, and all other attempts since that time to institute the use of school reports rather than examinations (see, for example, the 1947 Report of the Secondary Schools Examination Council, the Crowther Report, 1959; Schools Council, 1975; Broadfoot, 1979c).

Instead, 1917 saw the formal legitimation of academic school examinations in the establishment of the School Certificate. The new examination was a group certificate requiring passes in five or more academic subjects drawn from each of four groups of English, languages, science and mathematics, with music and manual subjects a fifth optional group. Thus the new Certificate established incontrovertibly the primacy of academic subjects and formal written assessments, relegating the aesthetic, practical and non-cognitive aspects of schooling to the relatively low status which still endures today (see pp. 75–6). It is significant, as the Beloe Report (1960) points out, that although the Secon-

33

dary Schools Examinations Council was set up at this time to advise the Board in maintaining standards, thereby ensuring some degree of State control over the content of education even at this relatively early stage of 'secondary' education, the universities were recognized as the appropriate bodies to conduct secondary school examinations and it is to them that we must attribute much of the emphasis in examinations on intellectual attainment and academic subjects. It is hardly surprising that the traditional pinnacles of the education system which had for long been the almost exclusive monopoly of the elite should be given the task of determining the structure of the newly emerging mechanisms of social selection. Nor is it surprising that they were determined in that elite's own interest.

In fact the elite schools could and did continue to stress the Victorian virtues of honour and leadership since, as Bourdieu and Passeron (1976) have argued, a variety of informal social advantages makes them less dependent on examinations for maintaining occupational status. For the rest of the population, the route to success now lay almost exclusively via examinations, either in winning one of the increasing number of free-place scholarships to the grammar school or, once there, in doing well in Lower and Higher School Certificate. Dore (1976) cites an interesting result of the change in the content of education we have been discussing. He identifies changes in the guides to various professions, such as journalism, which in 1900 emphasized the various qualities of character required for the job but which in 1950 specified only the formal academic qualifications required, as evidence of 'the slow change in Britain's mechanisms and criteria for job selection ... with the emphasis slowly shifting from personal aptitude to quantitatively measurable educational achievement'. As a result, 'the social definition of the purpose of schooling changed and with it the motivation of students and the quality of learning'.

Indeed another aspect of this change in the 'quality of learning' concerns the kinds of competency rewarded by examinations. The Consultative Committee Report of 1911, in discussing the effects of examinations upon pupils, pointed out that examinations place a premium on the reproduction of knowledge, passivity of mind and a competitive or even mercenary spirit and by contrast, do not encourage independent judgement, creative thinking, true learning and criticism. Although educationists have consistently deplored this constraint on genuine learning, all the evidence is that it will continue and in fact increase (Fairhall, 1978). There are links here with the importance of assessment as a means of social control, because the encouragement of passivity and acceptance of prevailing knowledge, values and standards and the restriction of entry to elite positions to those willing to conform to such definitions, are vital aspects of the process of social reproduction. It was by no means accidental that this kind of learning came to be emphasized in schools, for indeed it was regarded as essential that mass schooling should not be such as to allow people to question their station in life or the standards laid down by their betters, but rather serve to induce a greater degree of orderliness, morality and diligence. This straitjacket was very conveniently provided by the form and content which came to characterize school examinations and to this day restricts the acquisition of school qualifications to those willing to accept the values of the school and passively to reproduce existing forms of knowledge (Keddie, 1971).

Competition

The rapidly expanding economy of early nineteenth-century England depended not only on the discovery of new techniques and the creation of new markets; it required too a new type of worker who was prepared to sell his labour in return for money. The decline of the family as an economic unit of production and the concomitant rise of individualism coincided with the need in the economy for a new class of more scientifically educated managers; thus schools were increasingly looked to as providers of individuals with the requisite knowledge and skills (Musgrave, 1968). The rash of public schools founded at this time, particularly in the 1840s of which Marlborough, Wellington and Rugby are amongst the most well-known, was the direct result of the simultaneous influence of both the old social tradition whereby the more successful bourgeoisie sought to acquire for their sons the training of a gentleman, and the beginning of a new emphasis on *educational* capital which was subsequently to be of great significance. It was not to be long before the impecunious members of the elite began to realize that their sons might maintain their political and economic status by means of the acquisition of educational qualifications.

So rapidly did the emphasis on educational qualifications for entry to occupations grow, however, at the expense of the more traditional methods that it was not very long before the pressure on entry to many of the professions made selection imperative and gave schools a new role in preparing and adjudicating between candidates for an increasing variety of occupational roles. The result was that schools at all levels — elementary, grammar and public — began to place a growing emphasis on competition. The importance of education now as a path to *acquiring* social status led the universities also to recognize the need for some mechanism to regulate the new competition (Roach, 1971). Thus, as a result of the 1850 Oxford and Cambridge Royal Commission, in 1857 and 1858 respectively these universities set up School Examination Boards to provide a link with the increasing number of middle-class schools and hence with the new industrial and professional sections of society. The institution of entrance examinations by London and Durham universities at the same time was part of this trend.

An even more significant example of the trend towards a merit and achievement ethos at this time was the institution in 1855 of examinations for entry into the Home and Indian Civil Service after the model of those of ancient China. These examinations were significant not only as *qualifying* examinations but particularly for their emphasis on *selection*; in many ways they marked the translation of the capitalist belief in raising standards of production by competition to a similar philosophy for education (Lawson and Silver, 1973). In the increasing use of examinations to determine the awarding of scholarships and the allocation of vocational opportunity, we see not only the origins of 'criterion-referenced' assessment (Rowntree, 1977) — the measurement of specific competencies — we see also the origins of 'norm-referenced' assessment — the ranking of the performances of candidates one against another to determine the allocation of scarce resources. It was not very long before the use

36

of examinations to determine competence paled into comparative insignificance beside their use in selection, and the content of assessment often came to have little to do with the nature of the activity for which it was acting as a filter. School examinations, in particular, were prone to this lack of content validity, especially after the institution in 1917 by the Board of Education of the School Certificate, which put an end to school examinations linked to particular professions and replaced them with a standard school-leaving and university entrance qualification. School Certificate examinations have continued to be used as a selection mechanism for activities with which their content bears little relation; in many instances, research has shown them in fact to have a low or even negative correlation with vocational training or performance (for example, SCRE, 1976; Williams and Boreham, 1972).

Nevertheless, by 1922 and the establishment of the Higher School Certificate, a rationalized system of competitive, norm-referenced school examinations was firmly established through which all but a very few professional and academic aspirants must pass. It must be pointed out though that these examinations still combined a large measure of attestation with competition, in that with the huge gulfs between the elementary, grammar and public schools, the crucial determining point for career chances was still gaining entry to the grammar school or, even better, via the largely nominal Common Entrance Examination, to a public school. (The institution of this latter examination is another telling example of how prevalent the emphasis on overtly *educational* competition had become even if much more important selection devices such as family connections or wealth were still decisive covertly.)

However, after the institution of 'secondary' education for all in the 1944 Education Act and the raising of the school-leaving age to 15 in 1947, the *de facto* exclusion of the majority of children from the opportunity of taking School Certificate examinations could no longer be relied upon to limit competition. Thus, pursuing the philosophy expressed in their 1945 pamphlet 'The Nation's Schools', which stated the intention to 'free' the secondary modern school from the constraints of external examinations, Circular 103 in 1946 forbade schools other than grammar schools to enter pupils for School Certificate examinations below the age of 17, thereby re-establishing the pre-1944 situation by effectively debarring secondary modern pupils *de jure* from any opportunity to compete for formal educational qualifications.

Indeed the two themes of 'content' and 'competition' are inextricably interwoven in the development of School Certificate examinations. Concern over the domination of the curriculum by school examinations and arguments in favour of more school-based reporting had been continuously expressed since the Report of the Consultative Committee in 1911. The Spens Report in 1938 deplored the fact that 'despite all safeguards, the School Certificate examination now dominates the work of the schools, controlling both the framework and content of the curriculum'. In addition, Hartog and Rhodes' famous study in 1935 of the unreliability of examinations had added fuel to the fire. Indeed Lowndes (1969) argues that, had it not been for the Second World War, the School Certificate examination would have become a thing of the past to be replaced by a modified internal examination with national currency. In 1943 the Norwood Report spoke out against the reliance of examinations to motivate pupils when stimulus should have come from other sources, and they too proposed internal school assessment which would be a record of achievement in each subject but would not be seen as a predictor of future performance — or used as a mechanism of selection, a function which would be the preserve of the new, single-subject, 18+ examination. They regarded it as essential that the assessment at the end of general education be free from domination by the universities — a view which was reiterated in 1947 in the Report of the Secondary Schools Examination Council which argued that all forms of public examination should be kept till well after the compulsory school-leaving age so that education for the majority of secondary school pupils (some 80 per cent) could be freed from external academic constraints with assessment being confined to the use of objective tests and school records alone. Circular 205 reiterated these proposals in 1949.

It is possible to regard the debate about opening up access to the School Certificate examinations as a clear example of the contradiction between the liberation and control functions of assessment identified in chapter 1. At one level, many educationists, then as now, deplored the constraining influence of external examinations and genuinely hoped to liberate schooling for the majority of pupils who could not hope to succeed anyway. On another level, it is possible to see beneath these 'liberal' ideals a very convenient argument for the restriction of access even to compete for the passports to high occupational status and thus a restriction of 'competition' to those (predominantly middle-class) pupils who managed to pass the 11+.

By the early fifties however, the great pressure from the secondary moderns for access to an external examination combined with the need for ever finer discrimination amongst certificate candidates themselves, resulted in the institution of the General Certificate of Education, Ordinary and Advanced Level in 1951. This new, non-grouped Certificate had the apparent advantages not only of allowing more flexibility in the curriculum, but also allowed a greater proportion of pupils some hope of success in at least one subject. It had the advantage too of both allowing secondary modern pupils to compete and still, because of its higher standard than the old School Certificate, effectively preventing open competition (Rubinstein and Simon, 1969). In fact the new examination was yet another example of the paradox inherent in the functions of educational assessment. On the one hand it created an ostensibly greater opportunity in allowing more pupils to achieve external certification and in so doing, kept motivation and conformity to the system high — as demonstrated by the ever-increasing number of entries. But it also allowed a more finely divisive ranking of achievement, in terms of the number and status of subjects passed as well as the grades achieved in each. It is arguable that the finer differentiation and greater specialization provided for by the new examinations, whilst apparently better serving the economy in its increasing need for different kinds of expertise, created a 'division of labour' among pupils which had important repercussions for social reproduction.

Firstly, as Bowles and Gintis (1976) argue in relation to the employment market, it allowed a situation of 'divide and rule' —

a fragmentation which prevented the formation of united, self-conscious disaffected groups in the education system. Secondly, taking Bourdieu and Passeron's (1976) argument, it allowed the elite to reproduce itself by identifying the more abstract and esoteric subjects which formed part of their traditional culture as 'hardest' and thus of the highest status academically. Thus in these subjects, by virtue of the particular linguistic and intellectual skills developed by their home background — defined by Bourdieu and Passeron as 'cultural' capital — the elite are enabled to perform better than pupils from other backgrounds, so that success in these subjects has a greater commodity value in the university and job markets. There is a good deal of contemporary evidence to substantiate this argument. Nuttall, Backhouse and Wilmott (1974) for example, found English language and literature and possibly Art was consistently leniently graded and Chemistry and French marking consistently severe in both CSE and GCE examinations with Physics, too, being severe in GCE and Maths at CSE. Kelly (1976), in a Scottish study, substantiated these findings for the Scottish O-grade examinations, noting in particular the extremes of the continuum which were modern languages at the end of maximum difficulty and home economics and metalwork at the other. Even more significantly, Kelly points out that 'pupil ability tends to cluster in academic or non-academic subjects with grouping of presentations tending to follow ability clusters — so that there are, in a sense, two certificates of unequal value'. Indeed, it does not require a research project to reveal that Physics O-level is commonly regarded as more difficult than Needlework because fewer people pass in it!

With all their manifest disadvantages, the central role of external examinations in determining career opportunities made it impossible for the secondary modern schools to remain uninvolved in the competition, for not only did parents and pupils push for at least the chance to compete, the status and morale of the school itself became increasingly dependent on how well its pupils did academically, in a vain imitation of the traditionally high status grammar school. Indeed so powerful was the lure of external qualifications that the idea of a radically different type of 'modern' school envisaged in the 1944 Act never had a chance.

Thus, by 1955 half the secondary modern schools were preparing pupils for external examinations such as those of the Royal Society of Arts and the College of Preceptors and indeed in 1954, some 5,000 pupils were entered for the GCE O-level itself. As the secondary moderns became increasingly geared to the small minority retaking the 11+ or 12+ and other external examinations, their organization and curriculum reflected ever more closely that of the grammar school. As a result, the secondary modern school could scarcely avoid regarding itself as a second best and the pupils regarding themselves as failures for not having passed the 11+. Partridge (1968), in his description of a secondary modern school, describes the preoccupation of the boys with passing examinations to the exclusion of any valuing of education for its own sake and he argues that giving opportunity to a few to compete for external examinations inevitably ruins the educational experience of the majority. R.H. Tawney (1951) described this as the 'tadpole' philosophy — that the unhappy lot of tadpoles is held to be acceptable because some tadpoles do in the event become frogs. Hargreaves' (1967) study of boys in a secondary modern school provides graphic testimony to this. Yet it would be hard to argue against giving the maximum number of pupils at least the chance to compete in the system and there can be little doubt that the move to extend the opportunity to sit for public examinations to the secondary modern schools was strongly endorsed by most liberal educational reformists. Indeed, the grip of the liberal ideal of opportunity on the education system had become so strong that despite these problems, demand for the extension rather than the abolition of the public examination system multiplied during the fifties. The Beloe Committee, set up in 1958 to investigate the possibility of such an extension, reported in 1960 in favour of a new 'Certificate of Secondary Education'. In their view an extension of the public examination system was inevitable. The 'CSE' instituted in 1965 was designed to provide the goal of a pass in at least one subject for about 60 per cent of the year group, the top band of the CSE being equivalent to an O-level pass. Thus once again, the public examination system was redesigned to prevent too great a build-up of frustration which might threaten the meritocratic system. The provision of an educational goal designed — as in the case of O-level — to be achieved by some 20 per cent of a year group only — was already an anachronism in 1951, after the creation of universal secondary education in 1944. The creation of the CSE allowed far more, if not all, pupils to participate in the race without any serious threat to the reproduction mechanisms of the system. The social significance of the CSE, its innovation of new mechanisms of public examinations by the creation of three different 'modes' (Hoste and Bloomfield, 1975), the more recent proposals to reform both 16+ and 18+ examinations and the leading role taken in these developments by the Schools Council on Curriculum and Examinations, set up as a teacher-controlled body in 1964, are very much symptomatic of contemporary trends in assessment internationally and thus we shall leave them to the next chapter.

Control

Our final theme in the development of educational assessment is its function as an agent of social control. In many ways this whole book is about social control — and the way the educational system is made responsive, through assessment practices, to the prevailing power structure and economic and social conditions.

The question of control may be readily divided into two related issues — the control of the school *system* — particularly with regard to curriculum and organization, to ensure the production of suitably trained and socialized people to meet the needs of the economy on the one hand and, on the other, the control of individuals in ensuring they remain committed to the *status quo* and accept their own successes and failures in relation to the rewards of the educational system as just.

Selection and control

Musgrave (1968) argues that the radical economic changes in the mode of production which, as we have seen, had such a profound impact on education in the nineteenth century, resulted inevitably in a change in the basis of class divisions which in turn required the elite to find a new way to maintain and justify its privileged position. Indeed, so much did the social changes of the nineteenth century — social and geographic mobility, urbanization, bureaucratization, economic expansion — create pressure on all the various rungs of the educational ladder, that the scholarship and certification systems of selection alone would very soon have ceased to be an adequate way of regulating access to educational and vocational opportunity, had not another mechanism of legitimating selection been found to disperse the accumulating popular frustration. The pressure from those anxious to climb the rungs of the ladder was reinforced by pressure from those espousing the developing educational ideologies at the time. Williams (1977) has identified these various causes as the 'industrial trainers', the 'old humanists' and the 'public educators' but whether their concern was to make the maximum use of 'the pool of ability' by the institution of what Beatrice and Sidney Webb termed a 'capacity catching' machine or whether it was to promote social justice and social order, the effects were the same — a search for an accurate and thus fair way of identifying talent and of discriminating among pupils on purely educational, rather than, as had previously been the case, on social grounds. From these ideological and pragmatic pressures, the concept of the 'meritocracy' was born, a lusty infant which quickly came of age to dominate educational thinking virtually unchallenged to this day.

The search for some means of implementing this apparent meritocracy, of finding some means of objective measurement of merit, was not to be a protracted one. The solution, like the problem, was found in the new individualist emphasis in education which was in itself the underpinning of the meritocracy. A growing interest in *individual* achievement had led many nineteenth-century psychologists to study the determinants of various personal characteristics. Gradually, with the work of scholars like Galton and Spearman, there developed a conviction among psychologists that the determining factor in an individual's scholastic achievement was his innate ability or 'intelligence' — a quality that was both fixed and measurable. In addition, studies arising out of Binet's early twentieth-century

43

work in France with 'slow learners', such as Burt's (1912) article in England, 'The Inheritance of Mental Characteristics', and the widespread and apparently effective use of such tests by the United States army in 1918, quickly convinced academics and laymen alike that not only was it possible to measure 'intellectual ability' objectively but that from these measurements, *future* academic and occupational performance could be accurately predicted. 'To the scholars and men of science of the Victorian era, imbued as this era was with the spirit of the physical sciences, the thought that qualities as intangible and insensible as "intelligence" . . . could be accurately measured was revolutionary indeed' (Williams, 1974). Nevertheless, by the mid-twentieth century, so firmly established had 'intelligence' testing become that it dominated educational thinking. Sir Cyril Burt was for many people merely stating the obvious when in 1933 he wrote:

> By intelligence the psychologist understands inborn, all round intellectual ability. It is inherited, or at least innate, not due to teaching or training; it is intellectual, not emotional or moral, and remains uninfluenced by industry or zeal; it is general, not specific, i.e. it is not limited to any particular kind of work, but enters into all we do or say or think. Of all our mental qualities, it is the most far-reaching; fortunately it can be measured with accuracy and ease.

It is not hard to account for the rapid establishment of intelligence testing. It must indeed have been seen as an answer to prayer that, by means of a simple test, children could be readily and justly identified as 'bright' or 'dull'; their future predicted and, on this basis, categorized into different channels of the educational system. Not only that, but the scientific, 'objective' nature of such tests, their proven predictive power (Kamin, 1974) and their measurement of a characteristic believed to be as inborn as eye-colour, meant it was almost impossible for the recipient to reject the diagnosis. Thus intelligence testing, as a mechanism of social control, was unsurpassed in teaching the doomed majority that their failure was the result of their own inbuilt inadequacy.

No less significant than the use of 'intelligence' testing in scholarship examinations and other individual hurdles, was the rationale that the concept of fixed, innate capacity provided for the development of differentiated schools; indeed a great deal of the twentieth-century history of innovation in educational provision can be attributed to its influence. 'It was the conviction that children can and should be classified at an early age, according to inborn intellectual differences that underlay the entire remodelling of the school system at this time' (Rubenstein and Simon, 1969). From the Hadow Report (1926) onwards when the setting up of a system of separate schools to provide post-elementary 'secondary' education for all was first mooted, the doctrine of 'selection by differentiation' took over from that of 'selection by elimination'. During the next decade the 'intelligence' testing movement was to go from strength to strength. Thus by 1938 the Spens Report, in recommending a tripartite 'secondary' school system, could say with conviction, that 'with few exceptions,' it is possible at a very early age to predict with some degree of accuracy 'the ultimate level of a child's intellectual powers'. As a result, the few dissident voices, which included the TUC and the teachers' unions, arguing for a common (if internally divided) multilateral 'secondary' school, were drowned by the tidal wave in favour of separate schools designed to cater for children with different types of ability and inclination. This tide found its expression in the Norwood Report of 1943 and the Education Act of 1944 which enshrined the principle of education according to age, aptitude and ability and led to the establishment of the 'equal but different' secondary 'grammar', 'technical' and 'modern' schools which between them would provide for the new commitment to mass secondary education.

Nor was the influence of the concept of differentiated and fixed innate ability confined to the provision of three distinct types of secondary education alone. The 11+ examination which included tests of English and Maths as well as of intelligence, just as formerly the scholarship examinations for entry into grammar school had done, was in fact only an arbitrary cut-off point in a much longer process of categorization and channelling which became increasingly the norm in both primary and secondary schools. Many of those who rejected the idea

45

of differentiated secondary schools on the grounds of their being socially divisive accepted the need for differentiation within them. Indeed this view was supported by the continuing influence of the child-centred movement which was informing both a philosophy and a psychology of education emphasizing the importance of responding to the differing needs and interests of individual children. As early as 1926, after the publication of the Hadow Report, a great deal of effort was put into providing both senior and junior schools in which there could be three or more parallel classes to provide suitable learning environments for children of differing 'ability'. After 1944, 'streaming' in the primary school was common from the age of seven onwards, to give 'bright' children the maximum chance of developing their abilities and passing the 11+. The constraining effects of the 11+ examination on the work of the primary school was to figure prominently in the movement for its abolition during the next decades. Significantly for our theme of social control, it is this very liberation of the 'post-Plowden' primary school freed by and large from the constraints of the 11+ that lies behind a good deal of popular concern about 'falling standards' and the pressure towards the institution of new mechanisms of control — that is to say, accountability.

The secondary moderns too, catering for perhaps 75 per cent of the year group, soon took to streaming so that able pupils might have some chance of transferring to the grammar school or later, of GCE success. The result, compounded as we have seen by the effects of the competition for external examination certificates, was to effectively preclude any independent ethos of curriculum and evaluation developing in the secondary modern school, and hence, as Partridge (1968) asserts, the 'sacrifice [of the] long-term interests of the children who were likely to remain in the school throughout their school days to the overriding priority of the transfer out of the school of a few pupils'. However, the provision for even a very small number of secondary modern pupils to transfer to grammar schools or to sit for external certificates (still only 1 in 8 were sitting for GCE by 1960), allowed the belief in the system's capacity to identify and respond to ability at every level to persist. It encouraged confidence that the educational system was genuinely meritocratic in that for those few pupils who as late developers or for some other idiosyncratic reason had not demonstrated their ability early on in their school careers, the door to opportunity was never shut.

During the 1950s the concept of 'intelligence' as fixed and inherited gradually became untenable, as a result of a series of research studies (e.g. Halsey and Gardner, 1953; Yates and Pidgeon, 1957; Simon, 1953) which showed amongst other things the social class and environmental influences on 'intelligence' and that the IQ of pupils in grammar schools improved whilst that of their counterparts in secondary modern schools deteriorated. Such studies did little to attack the idea that it was possible to measure 'intelligence' objectively however, but rather fuelled the fires of those who believed that 'intelligence' was determined by environment rather than heredity and that some pupils were being prevented from developing their full potential by various kinds of disadvantages in their home background, such as coming from a large family, or having parents with low aspirations (Douglas, 1964). The result was, on the one hand, pressure towards 'compensatory' education which found its major expression in the Plowden Report's (1967) recommendation for the establishment of Educational Priority Areas. Schools in these 'deprived' areas would receive additional funding to help them overcome their pupils' background disadvantages. On the other hand, there was a parallel pressure against selection for secondary schools which could no longer be justified on the assumption of fixed and differing levels of intelligence. An NFER study in 1957 (Vernon, 1957), for example, showed that 122 pupils out of every thousand had been wrongly assessed in the 11+. Thus the pressure for a common non-selective secondary school which would allow much more flexible provision for different abilities and interests — a pressure which had been eclipsed by the rival ideology of selection in the 1940s — became increasingly intense until finally incorporated as government policy, in the commitment to comprehensive schools expressed in the famous Government Circular 10/65 of 1965.

In fact the change of policy from selective to comprehensive secondary education is yet another example of the complex system of checks and balances which operates to preserve the

47

social order through education. Certainly by the 1960s, it was no longer possible, as it had been earlier, to shut out large sectors of the population from the opportunity to compete for educational qualifications. However, 'the grading of children by ability (streaming and setting), the structuring of curriculum subjects into age-related blocks, assumptions about learning, motivation and teaching style, even the physical design of classrooms, meant the impossibility of thinking about education except in these ['intelligence' testing] terms' (Esland, 1977). Thus although the comprehensive school apparently provided open opportunity, in practice, as we shall see in more detail in chapter 5, the notion of differentiated ability still predominated, allowing selection to continue as before but in a much more acceptable guise.

It is the continuing class bias in educational achievement (Halsey, 1978), despite all apparent efforts to overcome it through compensatory education, comprehensive schools and curriculum reform, which has led sociologists of education in recent years to leave the squabbles over the hereditary versus environmental effects on intelligence to the psychologists and to examine, by disputing the apparent objectivity of intelligence testing, the role such testing may have played in perpetuating class differences in educational achievement. It may well be argued for example, that only the advent of intelligence testing made possible a 1944 Education Act which was a 'looking-glass' image of mid-Victorian assumptions (Maclure, 1965) in its provision for three distinct educational routes which were an exact replica of those recommended by the Taunton Commission nearly a century earlier in 1868. Thus it may well be argued that 'IQ' provided for the twentieth century the selection that wealth and breeding provided for earlier times, obscuring rather than abolishing the class influence on educational success. That is to say: 'the educational system legitimates economic inequality by providing an open, objective and ostensibly meritocratic mechanism for assigning individuals to unequal economic positions (Bowles and Gintis, 1976). R.H. Tawney put the idea rather more pungently as 'the impertinent courtesy of an invitation offered to unwelcome guests in the certainty that circumstances will prevent them accepting' (Tawney, 1951). Chomsky

(1977) asserts that the ability of intelligence testing to *obscure* the perpetuation of class inequalities (which it did successfully for nigh on fifty years) has been one of its most important functions, for 'intelligence' tests served 'to so mask power as to effectively immobilize any real revolutionary opposition' (Bacharach and Baratz, 1962). Not only was the widespread trust in this apparently objective measurement of potential sufficient to ensure that once assessed, 'the effect of differential expectations was sufficient to make that assessment come true' (Karier, 1973), the very content of the tests may be argued to favour the dominant class.

Westergaard and Resler (1975) argue that although it was increasingly necessary from the late nineteenth century onwards to expand educational provision and opportunity so that the growing technical and managerial posts in the economy could be filled, it was no part of the plan that 'children from privileged homes should be thrown into competition with working-class children to sink, swim or fly on "merit" alone'. Rather 'the putting into practice of the conception of intelligence, acted to *control* social mobility in such a way that only those acceptable to the middle class would become mobile' (Henderson, 1976). That is to say, the middle class were not better able to *acquire* intelligence but to *define* it according to their own characteristics. Bourdieu has perhaps done most to clarify this idea in his concept of 'cultural capital'. Since we shall discuss this more fully in chapter 4, it is sufficient at this stage merely to present his argument that the middle classes, finding themselves unable to perpetuate their status through 'capital' alone, were able to fall back onto a second line of defence— a school system which, though apparently allowing equal opportunity, was geared to the cultural mores of the ruling class and thus allowed them to perpetuate their privileged position by giving them a head start towards success in the education system.

There has been a good deal of debate over the extent to which tests are in fact biased. There is evidence to support the view (Giles and Woolfe, 1977) that intelligence tests, particularly the non-verbal variety, are typically less biased in favour of the middle classes than other kinds of assessment such as essay-tests or teacher-ratings. Other writers have argued that the questions in intelligence tests are indeed biased by drawing on cultural knowledge more readily available to some sectors of society than others, so that in fact 'the tests measure only whether one has learned and believed what [the test-setters] have learned and believed. To the degree that one has, one may reasonably look forward to enjoying the kind of success that the [test-setters] enjoyed. The assumption that one who has not learned these things was prevented from so doing by bad blood is both gratuitous and self-serving' (Kamin, 1974).

The significance of such tests may lie less in any inherent bias but rather in their confirmation of intelligence as the key variable in school success. The scientific aura surrounding these tests was highly instrumental in hiding any hint of class bias in the very definition of what should constitute educational achievement. It is the ability of the middle class to select (if unconsciously) the criteria by which to judge intelligence 'in their own image' and then to effectively exclude questions about the class-linked nature of 'intelligence' from the arena of debate, which may be said to allow the perpetuation of the class system (Henderson, 1976). These important questions about class cultural bias in the organization and definition of knowledge itself are however beyond the scope of this chapter and we merely raise them here to link the historical developments discussed in this chapter with the more theoretical discussions of chapter 4, when we shall return to them in more detail.

Accountability and control

Finally, in our consideration of the origins of assessment practices, we shall consider the control exerted by assessment on the educational system itself rather than on the individual within that system and in particular the way in which schooling is made responsive to the needs of the economy.

Before the mid-nineteenth century, the concept of accountability would have had little meaning in the context of the largely *ad hoc* educational provision of that time. As the century grew older however, it became increasingly apparent that voluntary agencies and in particular the Church, could no longer provide schooling on the scale necessary to train and control the masses for the new industrial society in which so many of the old skills and old social codes were being swept away. We have seen too that this was the time when the privileged sections of society were having to resort to schooling as the new means of perpetuating that position of privilege that land and money could no longer ensure. Thus it was necessary both that the State should provide at least an elementary education for the masses in order that they should acquire both relevant skills and appropriate work and social disciplines, and that the State should be able to control the amount and content of the schooling available according to the needs of the economy and the funds available. It is hardly surprising that initially, the means of control chosen — the 'Revised Code' that came to be known as the 'payment by results' system — corresponded exactly to the cost-effectiveness principles characteristic of business at that time — 'a logical development of the Benthamite idea in subjecting education to the yard-stick to which the Victorian expected his business to be subjected' (Midwinter, 1970). In Robert Lowe's famous words, a system which ... 'if it is not cheap, it shall be efficient and if it is not efficient, it shall be cheap'.

The system required the overall level of school grants — from which teachers were paid — to be dependent on the proficiency of individual children in meeting the standards laid down for the various grades. The effect of the 'Code', which encouraged drilling, rote-learning, and frequent testing in the three 'Rs', to the exclusion of almost every other aspect of the curriculum, academic or social, was to last for generations. Although providing less overt emphasis on character training than the schooling of the early part of the century, the system provided an excellent example of what Johnson (1976) has called the 'cul-de-sac of skills' in its emphasis on the unquestioning and diligent application of pupils to the learning of very basic skills. As such it was also another manifestation of the kind of control external examinations were already encouraging in restricting learning to memory and repetition rather than creativity and criticism. The Code was also indirectly significant in two further ways. Firstly it reinforced the trend in all types of school towards a greater stress on assessment by implying that the outcomes of education could and should be measured and by implication, reinforced the growing emphasis on academic rather than non-cognitive development by implying that outcomes of education not amenable to systematic measurement were not important — a view that is still prevalent today (Broadfoot, 1978a). Secondly, it initiated the concept that accountability for the use of public funds could and should be reckoned in terms of the academic performance of the scholars.

The gradual decline in the importance of the system towards the turn of the century was the result of many factors — not least the growth of the teacher unions and the need for ever greater curricular diversity. It was also made possible by the concomitant growth in public examinations which acted as 'quality-control' devices by restricting access to various points in the occupational hierarchy to those with proven competence. The pressure to gain such qualifications was highly instrumental in ensuring the efficient functioning of schools. As early as the first half of the nineteenth century, Woodward and Brereton — two contemporary educationists — had recognized the power a system of external examinations would have to bring about curricular unity, common organization and a raising of standards in the teaching profession, whilst at the same time safeguarding the schools from State control as such (Roach, 1971). It is indeed no accident that England and Wales are characterized by one of the highest degrees of school autonomy and at the same time, one of the greatest preoccupations with public examinations of any country. As a result, 'good' schools tend to be identified as those with a good record of public examination passes and particularly a high proportion of entrants to the twin academic pinnacles of the education system — Oxford and Cambridge Universities. As a result, too, a 'good' teacher tends to be defined in terms of his or her ability to get pupils through public examinations. Combined with the fact that the various Examining Boards are dominated by personnel representing various established interests in society, such as the universities and the professions, the power of the public examination system to define and maintain standards in the interests of that 'establishment' is immense and all the more effective for being covert.

In chapter 3, in looking at contemporary international trends in assessment, we shall consider the recent international trend back to overt accountability measures once again. We shall consider this trend in the light of the declining acceptability of public examinations and thus the growing inability of the State to control the education system in those countries where administration is relatively decentralised.

In Britain, the Assessment of Performance Unit (APU) set up by the Department of Education and Science in 1975 to monitor national standards in the main areas of the curriculum, which is discussed in more detail in chapter 3, is an heir to the Revised Code of 1862, and in particular, to its post-1891 expression when it was converted to the examination of only a one-third sample of pupils for reasons of economy. The changed economic and social climate of today make it neither possible nor necessary to penalize individual teachers or schools for low standards, since public opinion and the internal pressures of the system are sufficient to encourage schools to 'toe the line'. It is indeed significant how similar the emphasis of this twentieth-century accountability mechanism is to that of the nineteenth, despite the incursions of decades of 'progressive' education, for although plans are already well advanced for monitoring standards in numeracy, language skills and science, there is more than a hint in the literature (APU, 1977) that the monitoring of the social, moral, aesthetic and religious aspects of the curriculum although proposed, may not be implemented. This may well be because consensus as to appropriate testing techniques and standards in the traditional subjects of the curriculum is a great deal easier to achieve than it is in the social, moral, aesthetic and religious domains which in an age of diverging values can rarely be agreed upon except in very general terms. Thus it seems likely that because of pragmatic limitations the APU will inevitably reinforce and legitimate, almost by default, definitions of educational competence which emerged in the very different economic and social climate of over a century ago

An equally interesting manifestation of this pendulum of accountability is in the current debate over criterion- and norm-referenced assessment (defined on page 36). In the 1860s it was possible to define specific criteria of attainment after the manner of 'to make out or test the correctness of a common shop bill'. The advantages of criterion-referenced assessment (Block,

1971) in eliminating the competitive element endemic in most educational assessment has been widely discussed in the contemporary literature on assessment (e.g. Popham and Husek, 1969; Bloom, 1971), as have its negative effects of 'teaching to the test'. Criterion-referenced tests were possible for the nineteenth-century elementary school, since their use was confined to an exercise of quality control, not selection. By contrast, when the scholarship examinations for entry to grammar school began in the 1870s, they had to be norm-referenced since success was limited to the number of scholarships available rather than to all those who could reach an agreed standard— if indeed a standard could have been agreed. (The effect, as I have argued, was much the same in both cases, though, since the existence of the sought-after scholarship examination ensured a high-degree of curricular control.) However, it is interesting that, as we shall also see in more detail in the next chapter, the wheel has now turned almost full circle. As a result of 'qualification inflation' (Dore, 1976) the young school-leaver of today, although older than the former elementary school-leaver, has probably very little more chance of social mobility through competing in the educational qualification race despite an apparently much more open system, and thus there is a declining need for *selective* assessment at this stage. Rather the current pressure in most educationally advanced countries is towards criterion-referenced tests at the end of compulsory schooling (Schools Council, 1975), which will ensure, as in the nineteenth century, that the State is getting value for the £1800 million — 6 per cent of GNP — it spends every year on education, in the production of a numerate and literate work force.

Summary

This has inevitably been a 'whistle-stop' tour of the development of educational assessment in England which, like all 'whistle-stop' tours, has perforce had to leave out many of the interesting diversions along the way. We have not been able for example to consider the development of assessment procedures which paralleled the establishment of the alternative educational routes in various kinds of technical and further education, all of which were significant in their own way. These have been deliberate sacrifices in order to identify the main threads underlying a variety of idiosyncratic developments and to show how these threads, interwoven in intricate and subtly balanced patterns, provide a series of different expressions of the same constant relationship between society and the economy on the one hand and education on the other, which is assessment. Thus we have seen how the initial Victorian concern to establish competence expanded to allow the measurement of degrees of competence and thus enabled assessment to play a crucial role in the gradual emergence of the meritocracy ideal, as England moved from a largely static society of traditional roles to an expanding and dynamic structure based on individual achievement. I have sought to show how assessment, and in particular intelligence testing, whilst nominally the key to the meritocracy, was also a highly effective means of obscuring the perpetuation of class privilege through the education system. Throughout the growth of the education system in the late nineteenth and twentieth centuries it has been possible to trace the contradictions inherent in the conflict between the ideology and the social function of the education system, to match the apparent expansion of opportunity with the development of increasingly subtle mechanisms of assessment which operate to reproduce the *status quo* and legitimate it as apparently meritocratic. I have argued a central role for assessment in the elevation of particular forms of knowledge and of particular ways of reproducing that knowledge. Perhaps most significantly we have seen how, through assessment, an apparently autonomous education system can be subtly and pervasively controlled by the powers that be in society. Many of these issues are highly controversial and the analysis of this chapter will have succeeded in its intention if it has done nothing more than justify a new set of parameters — competence, content, competition and control — with which to analyse the contemporary international developments in assessment to which we now turn.

3

International perspectives and trends

One of the many debts owed by contemporary sociology to its founding fathers — Marx, Durkheim and Weber — is their emphasis on studying social phenomena in an historical and international context. It is perhaps only with the growth of neo-Marxist perspectives in recent years that the importance of the *grande vision* has been re-established, along with the equally important in-depth insights of the 'new directions'. Certainly as far as assessment is concerned, to ignore the international context is to invite a very unbalanced and inadequate account of contemporary trends, for the issues that have dominated the debates on educational assessment in Britain in the last ten or fifteen years have been echoed in most, if not all, of the industrial and industrializing countries of the world. In France, Germany, Sweden, Denmark and the Netherlands and in the less developed countries of Europe, in the United States, the USSR and the Eastern bloc and in Australia — indeed in any country with mass and extended education the same answers to the same questions, the same dilemmas, are apparent. Herein too, lies the justification for excluding from this analysis of international trends in assessment the idiosyncratic educational problems of the Third World which space does not allow us to deal with separately. To the extent that such countries seek to emulate Western industrial society, and seek to engage in the world economy, they are likely to come to model their education systems in response to economic, social and political influences very similar to those affecting advanced industrial societies and — as Beeby (1966) has argued — go through similar stages of development. The strength of such international constraints is clearly demonstrated in the experience of a country such as China, which sought to establish a rather different overt social and political emphasis in her education system but is in fact increasingly constrained by economic pressures — as was pointed out in chapter 1 — to conform to international norms.

Assessment practices reflect and reinforce the often conflicting values embodied in the education system. Debates over the reform of assessment procedures frequently illustrate the tension that exists between, for example, educational goals defined by industry and those of teachers, or that conflict already identified between elitists and liberal reformers. As Forsyth and Dockrell (1979) suggest, assessment procedures are likely to change incrementally rather than radically as a result of a process of oscillation in the degree of influence which various bodies associated with the education system are able to exert at any one time — itself a product of changes in the social, economic and political climate. Thus to understand the changing issues in assessment, we must look, briefly, at recent international changes in the structure and function of schooling in response to changing educational ideologies and social conditions. To the extent that these changes are similar in different countries, they reinforce the importance of understanding education and, by definition, educational assessment procedures, in relation to the wider societal and indeed, inter-societal forces acting upon it, and hence of not over-estimating the internal autonomy and scope for change of any one education system.

Thus, in most industrialized societies today, it is possible to identify similar trends in educational assessment practices. To a greater or lesser extent, each is characterized by the extension of public assessment to all pupils up to the end of statutory schooling and a corresponding postponement of selection. Equally there is a common trend to more comprehensive assessment including a much wider range of behaviour than before with a corresponding decline in formality in favour of more teacher-based assessment techniques. Thirdly, and most recently, we are witnessing a renewed interest in accountability and the way assessment procedures may be used to monitor or even control the performance of institutions and the education system as a whole, as well as of individual students. We shall now examine each of these trends in turn and by so doing hope to illuminate two of the central themes of this book — the dynamic interrelationship between assessment procedures and changing social and economic forces and the series of checks and balances governing innovation in assessment procedures which ensures that the essential social functions performed by them — allocation and legitimation — are in no way threatened. The final section of the chapter offers a conceptual model of this relationship.

The postponement of selection

One of the most marked international trends in assessment concerns the postponement of selection. This trend is particularly marked in Europe where typically a tripartite division of secondary education has been or is being replaced by the provision of a common school for all children up to the end of compulsory schooling. The tripartite model of secondary schooling based on 11+ selection introduced in England in 1944 was typical of European practice at that time in providing prestigious academic institutions for the few, technical schools as a second best for some and extended elementary schools for the majority. Thus for example in the Netherlands, selection at twelve and a half years of age channelled pupils into the Lower and Intermediate General Secondary School (LAVO), the technically and vocationally oriented Higher General Secondary School or, for a favoured 4 per cent (in 1968), the university-oriented high school (VWO). In Spain, before 1970, pupils were selected at ten years of age either to continue their elementary education to fourteen or go into the secondary school until they were seventeen or more. In France pupils were divided between the collège d'enseignement générale, the collège d'enseignement téchnique and the prestigious lycée. Similar patterns could be found in most European countries until fairly recently in which the majority of children would be allocated at around eleven to a non-selective secondary school which they would expect to leave at the statutory leaving age with few or no formal qualifications. For the minority, there was the extended secondary school catering for perhaps 5-25 per cent of the year group and geared to university entrance, characterized by the widespread use of the name 'lycée' or 'gymnasium'. Until recently the culmination of such schools was an examination which was both necessary and sufficient qualification for university entrance. Thus the post-Second World War picture of school organization in Europe reflected a clear system of 'sponsored' mobility (Turner, 1960) with common education terminating well before the statutory school-leaving age and children being identified, apparently on merit, as future elite members, technocrats or semi- and unskilled workers at an early age.

Just as the origins of this system lie, as we saw in chapter 2, in the social and economic forces of the nineteenth and early twentieth centuries, so similar common social and economic forces are effecting a change in this structure although national ideals of educational practice are sufficiently powerful to account for important and distinct national differences in the rate and form of such change. The trend is by no means unidimensional. Thus typically now, selection is deferred at least to fifteen or sixteen at the end of compulsory schooling and increasingly to eighteen or nineteen when those continuing with their education divide once more into academic and technical/vocational routes, the third group entering straight into the labour market (if decreasingly into jobs). In 1946 the Report of a Royal Commission in Sweden proposed a new comprehensive 'grundeschule' for all pupils, thereby pioneering in Europe the model of non-selective schooling throughout the period of compulsory education — a model which was already established in the Soviet Union and the United States, perhaps because of a more long-standing preoccupation in these countries with education as a means of creating equality of opportunity and national unity, in contrast to the more single-minded European association of secondary schooling with academic excellence.

The social and ideological forces underlying the move towards comprehensive reform, which is indeed defined by the OECD as the 'postponement of differentiation', are immensely complex, the explanation of which for England alone has filled whole volumes (see e.g. Rubenstein and Simon, 1969; Benn and Simon, 1970). It is possible though to identify several specific influences which both arise from and in turn affect assessment practices in particular. One such is Dore's (1976) concept of 'qualification inflation'. The increasing expansion of educational provision (the reasons for which we explored in the context of England and Wales in chapter 2), he argues, allows more people to gain those qualifications which traditionally led to high-status jobs. Without an equivalent expansion in the number of such jobs, the result is a devaluation of qualifications and a raising of the 'rate for the job' on the classic 'supply and demand' principle with consequent pressure on the education system as students seek to obtain ever higher level qualifications. Thus in the United States for example the percentage of 18-21 year-olds enrolled in post-secondary educational institutions had increased from 20 per cent at the end of the Second World War to approximately 50 per cent in 1973 (US Bureau of Census, 1973). In Japan the numbers enrolled in higher education have doubled since the war and now over 90 per cent of pupils obtain the basic high school qualification and stay on beyond the end of compulsory education. In Norway, over 99 per cent now stay beyond the statutory leaving age and not only has university provision doubled, there are experiments with comprehensive 'post 19' education. In Britain, in 1963, 27,800 school-leavers entered degree courses but in 1973 the equivalent figure was 44,600. Similarly, the proportion of school-leavers with no formal qualifications dropped from 66.8 per cent in 1963 to 21 per cent in 1973. These and similar trends which could be identified in all advanced Western societies clearly testify to more and more pupils achieving qualifications at each level of schooling and hence to these qualifications having less and less value as selection instruments.

The postponement of the crucial point for selection is clearly evidenced by typical changes which have taken place in certification procedures — the formal expression of assessment at the termination of a particular stage of schooling. The stages of certification have traditionally been twofold. The first stage was usually for pupils of about sixteen and existed to select candidates for higher secondary schooling and to provide those leaving school at this stage with qualifications which would allow establishments of further education and potential employers to select their future technicians, clerks and trainees for various trades. In this category would fall the Mittlere Reife in Germany, the Brevet d'Etudes du Premier Ciècle (BEPC) in France, the Certificate of Elementary Education in Spain, the Slutbety in Sweden, the 'Attestation of Maturity' in the USSR and O-levels and CSE in England.

The second stage of certification has typically been at the end of secondary schooling, at the age of eighteen or nineteen, and like the Abitur in Germany, the Baccalauréat in France, A-levels in England and matriculation in Australia, is usually the crucial selection mechanism for higher education.

The European experience provides a useful case-study of the changes taking place in this model with the universalization of mass secondary education. Typically formal selection procedures for State secondary schools have now been abolished (although in Germany, in particular, the progress towards the comprehensive secondary school is making slow progress (Rowan, 1976)). Countries still vary considerably, though, in the emphasis they put on 16+ certification.

Thus, for example, in the USSR the 'Attestation of Maturity' examination at the end of compulsory schooling still determines access to the various forms of continuing education and, although largely school-based, is a relatively formal examination (Gloriozov, 1974). In Denmark, despite the widespread reforms in the school system since 1970, including the efforts by most of the recent social democrat Ministers of Education to abolish selection for upper secondary school, public preoccupation with standards and the maintenance of academic excellence prevented Ms Ritt Bjerregaard, the Minister of Education, from succeeding in her attempt in 1977 to abolish such tests. France has recently (1978) gone slightly further in abolishing formal tests of selection for entry into post-16 education for all but borderline and private school pupils (*Journal Officiel*, 1977; Dundas-Grant, 1975). In Norway, the Committee on Evaluation reporting in 1978 and in Sweden, the Commission on Marking which reported in 1977, both recommended the complete abolition of marks for formal assessment in the comprehensive school (Council of Europe, 1977, 1978).

More and more the mystique and ceremony, the fine grading, the formal external examinations which used to inhere in 11+ and later 16+ assessment, have been transferred to the higher school certification stage and even beyond. The 'old' model of higher school certification was typically a grouped certificate in which candidates had to pass in five or so subjects to 'matriculate' and gain the qualification which was both necessary and sufficient qualification for university entrance. Formerly, when selection had already largely taken place before this stage, the future elite had already been identified — as in Turner's (1960) 'sponsored mobility' model— certification at this higher school stage was more concerned with the attestation of achievement than discrimination. Now, where such examinations still exist, it is no longer sufficient merely to pass but to pass well. In Germany, for example, the grouped subject Abitur is carefully graded to allow university admission on a strict 'numerus clausus' basis (Dungworth, 1977). The inauguration in countries such as England of a single subject examination replacing the former grouped certificate is also significant. Partly this may be accounted for by 'qualification inflation' for, as the ultimate level of qualifications and thus of curricula rises, the *specialist* study which used to characterize post-graduate courses is adopted not only for undergraduate courses but even in schools. But it may be, too, that a single subject examination allows greater discrimination by including both horizontal discrimination between the value of subjects studied and vertical discrimination in the standard obtained. And yet, at the same time, it allows more people some chance of succeeding and thus fits better with the increasingly comprehensive intake of the upper secondary school. The proposal in England to introduce new sixth-form examinations — the Certificate of Extended Education, for less academic, seventeen-year-olds and the 'Normal' and 'Further', '18+' examinations to cater for a much wider spread of abilities than the existing A-level examinations (Schools Council, 1977) was a recent, if ill-fated, expression of this process.

Britain's preoccupation with public examinations is indeed an interesting manifestation of the important and close relationship between certification mechanisms and mechanisms of system control — accountability — represented diagramatically in figure 1 (page 70). The hitherto very informal methods of system control characteristic of all the education systems of the British Isles to a greater or lesser extent have resulted in their being much slower to respond to the pressures for change in assessment procedures which have led to the international trends we have been discussing. This is an important constraint on changes in certification procedures. Thus Britain is currently the only country in Europe still setting formal external examinations on a mass basis at 16+. Although the new GCSE to be introduced in England in 1985 will do nothing to change this, it is some evidence of the effect of 'comprehensivization' in allowing a much larger number of pupils than before to gain a qualification at least nominally equivalent in status to GCE O-level. In general though, the signs are that apart from countries like Sweden in which assessment has already become almost totally informal, Europe is tending to lag behind in a world trend against selection based on formal certification at even 18+, since in large areas of the world such as Australia and the United States, assessment is either based on internal school records or postponed completely until after the start of higher education. We shall return to this issue when discussing the increasing teacher involvement in assessment later in the chapter.

Thus, to summarize the argument so far, it is possible to identify a consistent international trend towards an ever later key point of selection with a concomitant decline in the formality and significance of assessments for certification prior to this stage, a trend which is logically implied by the equally consistent expansion internationally of educational provision and take up.

Although the expansion of educational provision has thus

inevitably postponed the point of formal selection and the ensuing 'qualification inflation' is tending to postpone it still further,
it is not safe to assume that this postponement of selection has
created in fact any greater equality of opportunity in relation to
social class than existed under the previous selective secondary
education system. Bourdieu and Passeron (1976) argue by
means of a complex statistical analysis that in France during the
growth in higher education provision in the 1960s, 'often inter-
preted as a democratization of admissions, the structure of the
distribution of educational opportunities relative to social class
did indeed shift upwards, but it remained virtually unchanged
in shape. In other words, the increased enrolment of 18-20
year-olds was distributed among the different social classes in
proportions roughly equal to those defining the previous distribution of opportunities…'. Bourdieu and Passeron also argue
that a similar pattern of development of educational opportunity
combining increased enrolment of all social classes, with stabil-
ity of the structure of disparities *between* the classes, can be
identified in most European countries such as Denmark, the
Netherlands and Sweden and indeed has similarly been identified in the United States (OECD, 1969). Eggleston (1979) has
shown that in England likewise, there has been little significant
change in the relative achievements of social classes since comprehensivization.

Thus it is arguable that the reorganization of schooling and
the postponement of selection, whilst freeing primary and
elementary schooling from the worst excesses of cramming for
the secondary school selection examinations, has done nothing
to alter the tendency of schools to confirm pupils in channels
according to their social class background. An alternative and
complementary explanation of the international trend towards
the postponement of selection is that selection has in fact merely
been disguised, in order to prevent socially disruptive resent-
ment and frustration among those who are early labelled failures
in a system which they are obliged to endure for an extended
period of time and which is apparently increasingly crucial in
the allocation of life chances in a socially fluid society. Whether
or not Jencks (1972) is correct in arguing that education is not in

fact a crucial determinant of occupational success— and there is little agreement on this— is less important than the fact that it is *believed* to be by pupils and their parents. A palpably class-biased, selective educational system is no longer politically acceptable, given the commitment to a meritocracy on both humanitarian and efficiency grounds which characterizes contemporary educational policy in both liberal democracies and communist societies. In chapters 4 and 5 we shall explore the argument in more detail of how, in Western education systems at least, the class biases inherent in the internal organization of the school in the practice of streaming and grading, in the curricula and language of the school, and in teacher expectations, probably perpetuate class divisions more or less as if children were actually divided into separate schools.

We can usefully pursue this argument of changes in assessment procedures as a means to reinforce social control rather than as a means of creating any significant change in the structure of opportunity by focusing in more detail on changes in the method and content of certification which are accompanying the changes in the structure of schooling we have been discussing. Or, to put it in terms of the parameters set out in chapter 1, the complementary changes taking place in the 'who', 'what' and 'how' of assessment practice simultaneously with those pertaining to 'when' and 'why' that we have already identified.

Assessment for all

Neave (1979) posits a law of educational development 'in which assessment for all constitutes a fourth stage in what might be termed "the universalization" of extended secondary education' after the three earlier stages of comprehensivization, the abolition of internal school differentiation in the form of tracks and streams, and the institution of a common core curriculum up to the end of compulsory schooling. Bearing in mind the foregoing arguments about the postponement of selection it is logical to predict that assessment during the compulsory comprehensive stage of schooling will take on a different form and function. This has indeed proved to be the case with assessment procedures more concerned with motivation and diagnosis than selection and applied to all pupils in a routine way now becoming the norm. Although strong arguments have been put forward in Britain to institute such an assessment procedure for all pupils (e.g. SCRE, 1977; Schools Council, 1975), Britain is almost unique in clinging to the idea that all children cannot be included in formal assessment procedures without a lowering of standards. Elsewhere examinations at the end of compulsory schooling have typically given place to a regular series of standardized tests, routinely administered to all children at certain points in their school careers (Neave, 1979). In France all children have at least their 'livre scolaire' or school record to take with them from school. In the United States all children have a leaving certificate which simply consists of a record of the courses the pupil has taken and the grades he has received (Maguire, 1976). In Norway and Sweden, assessment is a routine matter for all pupils, normed and standardized to allow teachers to gauge their pupils' progress in relation to that of the country as a whole.

The extension of formal assessment to all the members of a year group when all those children are obliged to be in school is not in itself particularly significant and is indeed on a par with the design of earlier certification procedures geared to a particular percentage of the year group when only that percentage was in school. The content, mode and purpose of the assessment is much more significant and to this we now turn.

Increasing teacher involvement in certification

It is significant that to the extent that school certificates have become devalued, teacher involvement in certification has typically increased. Australia provides an interesting case study. All 16+ certification in Australia has been teacher conducted for some considerable time and has now begun to reach the next stage (see fig. 1) of disappearing altogether. (This has already happened in New South Wales and South Australia in 1976 (Maguire, 1976).) Likewise, 17+ and 18+ certification, although varying from state to state, manifests the same trend of being allowed increasing teacher control as its significance decreases until it ultimately withers away. Thus in Queensland, for example, certification is based on a school assessment scaled according to the Australian scholastic aptitude test. In Western Australia, likewise, school assessments are used. In Victoria, as in New Zealand, the accreditation system is used which requires only pupils from non-accredited schools to take formal examinations. In 1973 the Campbell Report in the Australian Capital Territory recommended the use of continuous school assessment as the basis for certification. But the most extreme example of this trend is in Victoria where in 1976 teachers refused to conduct the matriculation examinations for university entrance (Hill, 1976). They felt a lottery was the only fair way of selecting students for university until sufficient higher education provision could be made — surely a classic manifestation of 'contest mobility' (Turner, 1960). Although our analysis here, for the sake of clarity, has been confined to the Australian situation, the ubiquity of this trend is evidenced by the developments in assessment practice in other countries already referred to in this chapter.

Thompson (1974) has explained this trend towards teacher-based certification as the result of an increasing level of public trust and confidence in schools and teachers. Worldwide concern about accountability (Marjoram, 1977) seems to deny this argument especially since we have known for a long time that teachers are as reliable in ranking pupils accurately on both specific abilities and non-cognitive qualities as are any other form of test. Rather, I would suggest the phenomenon can be explained in terms of legitimation. If the examination is of crucial importance for selection it must be invested with as much apparent objectivity, ritual and formality as possible so that, almost after the manner of a divine utterance and certainly in the same way as an intelligence test, the results and the failure which they imply for many candidates are accepted. As the qualification concerned becomes progressively devalued and thus less significant in the allocation of life chances, so it can more safely be left to the informal, more personal responsibility of the teacher. Such a move however, as figure 2 suggests, is likely to be accompanied by the institution of increasingly systematic expressions of accountability.

The changing content of certification

We turn now to the remaining question set out at the beginning of this section, which concerns what is assessed. The most significant trend in this respect is the re-emergence of non-cognitive characteristics for inclusion in formal assessment. In Denmark the U90 Commission, setting out the form of Danish education for the years up to 1990, has stressed the need to broaden assessment to include personal and social qualities (Central Council for Education, 1977). In France, the 'Haby' reforms of the 'livre scolaire' (although rescinded in 1978) were significant in including assessments on affective characteristics such as 'sense of responsibility' and 'team spirit'. In Sweden the new structure recommended by the Commission on Marking in which parents, teachers and pupils would be jointly involved in assessment, also recommends that non-cognitive aspects of a pupil's progress be taken into account along with academic achievements (Duckenfield, 1977). Norway too has made similar recommendations (Neave, 1979).

We saw in chapter 2 how in England this originally crucial non-cognitive aspect of schooling, particularly for the top (public) and bottom (elementary) ends of the educational ladder, was eclipsed by the meritocratic movements towards apparently more objective cognitive measures. The reason for the re-emergence at the present time of such assessment may be found in the experience of the United States where the inclusion of information about extra-curricular activities such as debating or sport, and personal qualities such as leadership and sociability, have always made the school record an important complement to the largely ungraded High School Certificate. King (1967) argues that schooling in the United States has always of necessity given highest priority to the need to socialize and weld into a social unit all the diverse cultures represented in its immigrants. The stress on democracy and patriotism in American schools as evidenced by, for example, the morning flag-raising ceremony, may be one of the reasons why one in five

American adults is functionally illiterate (Binyon, 1976). At the other end of the political spectrum though, communist countries such as the Soviet Union and China have clearly recognized the political and ideological conformity that can be reinforced by taking into account a very much wider range of information about pupils than simply academic attainment (Price, 1976, 1977). For, given the importance of assessment in the allocation of career opportunities, whatever is assessed will be reflected in both the formal and informal curricular activities of the school. Thus if pupils know for example that leadership qualities count towards their final assessment, they will tend to strive hard, and be encouraged by teachers to show such attributes.

The increasing use of informal descriptive records during the compulsory schooling stage, containing both cognitive and non-cognitive information, may be explained too by the orientation to a different kind of school-leaver than was traditionally the case with 16+ assessment, when it was aimed typically at the top, academic end of the year group. Much recent writing in the sociology of education has argued the primacy of the school's role, not in encouraging intellectual development, but in developing appropriate non-cognitive qualities and self-perceptions which will 'correspond' with the pupil's future occupational situation (see for example, Bowles and Gintis, 1976; Willis, 1977). Employers of the young school-leaver do not want high intellectual calibre for boring repetitive jobs. Indeed they would tend to see it as a positive disadvantage in that such people would be likely to become easily disaffected and thus disruptive. Rather they are looking for basic skills and a good character (Brown, 1975; SCRE, 1977). Even corporations looking for potential management trainees may rate personal qualities — especially capacity for commitment — higher than intellectual achievement alone. By including non-cognitive assessment more overtly in certification the inculcation of appropriate attitudes and behaviour, which has always been one of the informal effects of schooling, is reinforced. And indeed, if youth unemployment on a massive scale is here to stay — as seems likely — the development of appropriate personal skills and attitudes and the orientation of education and assessment not towards jobs and job selection but towards personal development and fulfilment, is all too necessary if large-scale social unrest is to be avoided.

Changes in certification – a dynamic model

It is time now to draw together the various trends we have been discussing into a coherent whole. Figure 1 sets out schematically the interrelationship between these trends.

competitive		non-competitive		
Public Examinations (externally set and marked)	Moderated School Assessment (scaling, item banks, moderation committees, etc.)	Attestation of course completion	Teachers' descriptive records	Pupil self-assessment
FORMAL external				INFORMAL internal

increasing public trust in teacher assessment
<-->

decline in importance of certification for selection
<-->

increasing importance of assessment to retain commitment
<-->

increasing importance of non-cognitive assessment
<-->

Fig. 1 The changing pattern of contemporary assessment at the end of compulsory schooling.

Note: Although the typical trend at the time of writing seems to be from left to right on the continuum, there are some indications, particularly in the Communist world, of a movement in the opposite direction, towards increasingly formal assessment. The diagram is best visualized as expressing a constant relationship between various forms of assessment, the particular point on the continuum being determined by the prevailing social, economic, political and ideological conditions at any one time in any one country.

Figure 1 sets out the changing social control role of assessment with the growth of mass secondary education. At the left-hand end is the traditional picture of certification, when the exigencies of open and fair competition increasingly inherent in the meritocratic ethos of schooling throughout the industrialized world after the Second World War, were most strongly felt at the point of selection for secondary school and then later, at the termination of compulsory schooling. Moving towards the right-hand end of the continuum we find the changes which are taking place in certification with the postponement of the key point of formal selection to 18+ and beyond. In place of the emphasis on formal, external, unquestionable assessment — essential where the determination of life-chances is at stake if disaffection is to be avoided — is a new emphasis on broader-based, teacher-conducted assessment which can allow a greater concern in assessment procedures with diagnosis and motivation. Although the stage of pupil self-assessment is still largely conjectural, it is logically implied by this trend since if pupils are given responsibility for monitoring their own learning, the degree of personal involvement they have in their learning and their commitment to it is likely to be maximized (Broadfoot, 1979a). Thus pupil self-assessment is likely to provide one of the most efficient modes of social control in the same way that Bernstein (1977) has argued informal pedagogy is most controlling by being most seductive.

However, the delegation of control over the content and form of assessment to teachers and perhaps before long to pupils, raises other, macro-problems of control. Although, as I have argued, such delegation may enhance *individual* commitment to the education system, it leaves problematic the control over the system itself. Thus we should add a third parameter to figure 1 which identifies the growth of a different kind of assessment in direct relation to the decline in external school assessment. This parameter is accountability — the means by which the controlling interests in society monitor the operation of the education system as a whole and make it responsive to the needs of society as they define them.

This relationship is depicted in figure 2 which shows an increasingly overt emphasis on accountability in proportion to

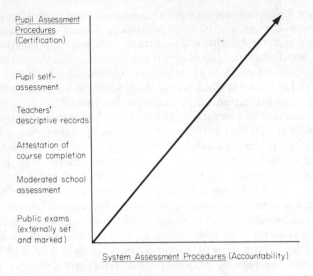

Fig. 2   Model showing overt accountability procedures as a function of declining public control of certification procedures

the decline of various degrees of control on pupil certification. For the sake of clarity, both figure 1 and figure 2 have been presented as linear models although it may well prove in the long run that a circular representation of the continuum would be more accurate. (See note p. 70.) The model is essentially an 'ideal type' — an abstraction which seeks to isolate trends from the complex and idiosyncratic interacting forces operating in any national education system — and thus doomed inevitably to over-simplify and to ignore specific anomalies in the general pattern. A consideration of contemporary trends in accountability does seem to emphasize however that the diagonal in figure 2 is a constant, in which any decline in external control on one axis is likely to be made up by a corresponding increase in external control on the other.

Accountability

The growing international preoccupation with 'standards' and accountability is perhaps most evident at the present time in the United States where national efforts to define and assess educational standards date back even to the halcyon days of 1964 when the tide of public opinion first began to flow strongly against liberal and progressive practices in education and in favour of more traditional pedagogy, discipline and testing. So strong has this concern with standards now become that by the beginning of 1978, 31 States had introduced some form of 'basic skills' testing in their schools and only 4 of the 50 States had no plans to do so. The scale of the movement is clearly shown by the fact that less than two years earlier, only 8 States required 'minimum competency' testing (Cookson, 1978). In California alone the Reform in Intermediate and Secondary Education movement (RISE), set up to ensure minimum standards of competency, will cost $200 million a year. In Oregon, Florida and Arizona, school-leavers must already demonstrate minimum standards before graduating (Binyon, 1976) and in some States, the controls are even more stringent in that grade to grade promotion within the school ceases to be automatic and is dependent on adequate performance.

There are echoes here of the worst traditions of the Victorian 'Revised Code' and of the typically European practice of children endlessly and often futilely repeating 'grades' they have not adequately mastered. Such a system is graphically described by the pupils of the Barbiana School in Italy in their *Letter to a Teacher*, in which they show that of the 454,094 thirteen-year-old Italians in school in 1969, 5 per cent were already in a scuola superiore, (to which pupils are supposed to transfer at fourteen) 33.9 per cent were in the third year (where they officially should have been), 28.7 per cent were in the second year and 18.2 per cent in the first year of the scuola media. The 13.9 per cent still in the elementary school, a third of whom had 'not yet reached the top class, must surely have been very disillusioned with education'! Although relatively educationally-backward countries like Italy are now abandoning this system, the wheel appears to be coming full circle in an increasing preoccupation with standards and a move away from progressive, child-centred ideologies.

In the USSR, not only are children required to repeat grades they have failed but there is an increasing emphasis, after years of ideological prohibition, on various kinds of formal testing (Ingenkamp, 1977). A similar situation is developing in China too (Bonavia, 1978). Denmark was typical of the European liberal democracies in passing an Education Act in 1974 emphasizing standards and formal testing and drastically redressing the balance against the earlier far-reaching progressive innovations in assessment instituted in 1972. The Netherlands, too, has almost reverted to a payment by results system in that State grants are only given to schools whose pupils can demonstrate acceptable standards in numerical and other basic skills (Maguire, 1976). Other countries are finding less obvious but nevertheless powerful modes of accountability. The new assessment system in Norway is designed to allow not only the monitoring of individual progress but indeed an evaluation of the performance of the institution itself by parents and pupils (Neave, 1979). In Sweden the nationally standardized tests used to scale internal school assessment and regularly administered to pupils have a triple function. They permit pupils to assess their progress and teachers to gauge pupil and class achievement against national norms. But they provide, too, detailed information on national standards and indeed a certain amount of curricular control as expressed in the nationally standardized tests of Swedish, mathematics, foreign languages, chemistry, physics, economics and accountancy (SED, 1977). Although 'accountability' to pupils and parents is less common than that oriented to government, the effect of both is likely to be substantially the same to the extent that parents and indeed pupils espouse the same goals for education as the system planners. Given the importance of assessment as a means of regulating life chances, the likelihood of parents and pupils emphasizing alternative goals to those implicit in formal assessment procedures is not very great. Thus it may be argued that in co-opting parents and pupils — who are often for this reason some of the more conservative participants in the education system — into the accountability process, the mechanisms of control over the education system, and teachers in particular, are in fact strengthened.

Britain has recently shown similar concerns over 'accountability' and has borrowed from American experience to set up a national 'Assessment of Performance Unit' (APU) not unlike the American National Assessment of Educational Progress (NAEP) programme. International interest has been shown in the Unit since it was set up by the DES in 1974 to identify and define, with a view to monitoring, standards in each of the major curricular areas, which have now been identified as language (native and foreign), mathematics, science, personal and social development, aesthetic development, and physical development (Marjoram, 1977). Two aspects of the APU's work are particularly significant. Firstly, it seems increasingly likely that although plans have been laid to assess all areas of performance, in practice progress is only being made with regard to languages, mathematics and science, 'the final decision on whether to include the [other] three aspects in a programme of monitoring has yet to be taken as there are major difficulties of assessment yet to be solved' (APU, 1977). A report in the *Times Educational Supplement* (27.10.78) confirms this. Dennison (1978) supports this view in arguing the total impossibility of defining aesthetic, moral or personal development adequately enough to assess it and, if it could be done, how clearly it would be seen as an infringement on personal liberty. (That so much of cognitive development is affected by non-cognitive factors is equally true but seems to cause less concern.) Certainly any assessment is an infringement on personal liberty but the result of *not* assessing important aspects of education such as moral and aesthetic development is likely to be a reinforcement of the neglect of these potential curricular areas brought about by their traditional, almost total exclusion from certification.

Thus it may well be that if the performance of schools is monitored only in the 'core' curricular areas, the effect will be not only to reinforce particular interpretations of what standards should be in these areas, but will also encourage a corresponding neglect of other, particularly non-cognitive, aspects of learning which, it has been argued, are currently receiving increasing emphasis in certification assessment. What the effect of this tension is likely to be it is too early to predict but it can be neatly characterized as a backlash against what Williams (1977) has termed 'the old humanists' and in favour of the 'public educators' and the 'industrial trainers'.

For an explanation of these somewhat contradictory trends we must turn once more to the dilemma identified in chapter 1 which underpins many of the analyses of this book, namely the so far insoluble problem of matching a liberal educational ideology with the need for social control, and social reproduction inherent in a stratified society. Thus the mechanisms that have been discussed for both individual and system control are, by their very nature, conflictual, since the needs of employers for a docile and relatively skilled work force do not match the emphasis on personal fulfilment and involvement in education which must be encouraged to maintain the commitment of individual pupils. At any rate the net effect of the APU monitoring is likely to be to cause schools perhaps even more than at present to be judged and to judge themselves in terms of their success in teaching the basic skills.

The second significant feature of the growing emphasis that we have identified, in some countries at least, on the closer monitoring and control of educational standards, is that the attribution of *responsibility* for pupil achievement may come to be seen increasingly in terms of the school rather than the individual pupil. Focusing once again on the English and American experience, since these two countries have taken some of the most overt measures in this respect, it is possible to trace a move away from the concentration on the environmental influences affecting the performance of certain class and ethnic groups which so preoccupied the Newsom and Plowden generations in Britain and the Coleman generation in America. This preoccupation has, in these two countries at least, faded in significance relative to the emphasis on *school* responsibility for pupil achievement. If this trend persists we may well see more cases like that in New Jersey recently, where a court upheld the petition of two parents against a school for the child's lack of achievement. The monitoring procedures are not normally set up in the first instance to evaluate individual schools. In England the APU proposes only 'light sampling'— only 1.7 per cent of selected age groups will be tested each year for each aspect of the curriculum, and all those tested will only take *part* of the total test so that comparisons between individual pupils are precluded. Eventually though the exercise is likely to involve a quarter of all primary schools and half of all secondary schools every year. Thus although the sampling is designed to preclude comparisons between schools as much as between pupils, and although the 'grapevine' and public examination results have already led typically to local identification of 'good' schools, it is not hard to envisage substantial public pressure to release a 'league' table of individual school performance, particularly in the case of junior and middle schools for which often little 'objective' data as to standards currently exists. This has certainly been the American experience. The *New York Times* publishes the city's 'League Table of School Attainments' without any qualifying information (Sherwood, 1978). Burstall and Kay (1978) describe the hostility and bitterness aroused in Michigan when the State educational authorities were pressured by politicians into releasing achievement test results for individual schools, having previously assured the teachers concerned that the results would be confidential — 'these results were published in local newspapers, giving rise to a "league table" of schools (apparently much in demand among the estate agents of the area), which took no account of the schools' differing human and financial resources. Teachers complained bitterly that the tests used did not adequately reflect the school curriculum, [and] that there had been little teacher involvement in the development of the tests . . .'. Although 'light' sampling as opposed to 'blanket testing' will probably postpone in England some of the problems condemned in the American National Association of Elementary School Principals' book *The Myth of Measurability*, we do not need to look beyond the Government's Green Paper of 1977 to see the dangers: 'It is an essential facet of their [Local Education Authorities] accountability for educational standards that they must be able to identify schools which consistently perform poorly, so that appropriate remedial action can be taken.'

Part of the explanation for the explosion of accountability programmes can certainly be found in the logical extension of principles of management control which are increasingly being incorporated into the school system (Timpane, 1976) — the increasingly formal division of labour and bureaucratic hierarchy in the school are obvious manifestations — which may be expressed in bald economic terms as 'getting value for money'. This analysis does not, however, explain the relatively sudden upsurge in public concern in this decade. The explanation is certainly enormously complex but once again may be found in the tension between the two conflicting goals of the education system with, in this case, the pendulum perhaps having swung too far in one direction. The 1960s had seen an international trend against elitism and towards the expansion of opportunity for all in education. It had revealed in many cases a liberalization of discipline; the increasing impact and radicalism of youth subcultures all over the world and a fashion for 'progressive' education. The effect of all these social forces was a major onslaught on the school's function as a socialization agency — as a mechanism for social control. Although the debate is ostensibly about 'falling standards' in terms of academic achievement, Burstall and Kay (1978) point out that the concern is a much broader one — at least in America — about the extent to which the educational system is successfully meeting the present and future needs of society. Public discontent focuses on both 'standards' and 'behaviour'. 'In fact the current educational debate in spite of all the concern for assessment of performance is not really about the measurable but about values' (Watts, 1978). It is thus certainly arguable that concern over supposedly 'falling standards' in England, for example — particularly in view of the (1978) HM Inspectorate report that standards in basic skills had if anything *improved* during the preceding years — is merely the tip of the iceberg of a much larger concern: that the decline of external examinations and the corresponding increase in the power of teachers to determine their own curricula and try out new 'progressive' methods, is making the education system increasingly autonomous. In particular, it may be argued, the innovations which characterized education in the 1960s, in challenging the traditional elitism, curricula, pedagogy and discipline of schooling, appeared to threaten the ability of the dominant social groups who had themselves set up this system to work in their own interest to reproduce the *status quo*. In particular the cold wind of economic crisis in the mid-seventies meant renewed pressure too for education to be as closely geared as possible to the needs of the labour market — as evidenced in the Prime Minister's speech at Ruskin College, Oxford in 1976 and the national debate that ensued.

We can substantiate this argument most easily by pursuing our case-study of assessment innovation in England in more detail. The Black Papers (Cox and Dyson, 1969a, 1969b, 1970, 1975, 1977) bear ample testament to the concern of certain sections of society over the apparent movement away from traditional curricula, pedagogy, discipline and internal grading practices in schools. To put this particular English example in context we must go back to where we left the development of public assessment in England at the end of chapter 2, the setting up of the Schools Council in 1964 and its associated development of the Certificate of Secondary Education (CSE) in 1963 — an examination designed to give maximum freedom to individual schools and teachers in curriculum and assessment. Both innovations were significant in ceding a substantial responsibility for the definition and control of educational standards to bodies dominated by teachers where before, through the Secondary Schools Examination Council, the DES itself had had close control over public assessment and thus educational standards. In addition, the existence of three different modes in the CSE greatly increased the number of syllabuses — as many as one thousand different papers in a single subject for a single board — thus preventing any close scrutiny of courses by the successor to the Secondary Schools Examination Council — the Schools Council — of either CSE or O-level syllabuses, unlike pre-1964 practice (Becher and Maclure, 1978). It is worth noting that the higher status A-level exams, which guard most closely the entry to elite status, are still controlled by the Schools Council in that all new or substantially-revised syllabuses must be approved by them. Becher and Maclure explain this change as the expansion of secondary education from elite to mass proportions which strained the traditional mechanism for central control of the public curriculum, for in England the external examinations have been one of the most crucial mechanisms of control in a highly decentralized system and their importance in this respect may be one reason why any attempt to reform or abolish them meets with a good deal of opposition and concern over the likelihood of thereby encouraging 'mediocrity'. Even the attempt to institute the relatively minor change of uniting GCE and CSE into a common system of examining at 16+ has taken eight years. In an era which requires prolonged 'elementary' (i.e. mass) schooling which is dominated by the ethos of meritocracy, it is no longer possible to deny the majority of school pupils a tangible goal in schooling, particularly when employers equally conditioned to the meritocracy ethos have learned to discriminate between applicants very largely on the basis of formal qualifications (Dore, 1976). It can be argued though that the international trend towards internally set school examinations (and, by implication, curricula) discussed earlier in this chapter, which was made possible by their declining importance for selection, brought with it unforeseen problems of control. England was rapidly approaching a situation in which teachers could decide what they wanted to teach, how they wanted to teach it and whether they had been successful, with little reference to any outside authority. Thus the dominant interests of the State were losing control of the most powerful agency of social reproduction. In view of the fact that as Raven (1977) has shown teachers value most highly the personal and social development of their pupils, it is not surprising that the more autonomous the school system, the greater the disparity between the emphases and hence achievements of schools and the demands of industry and the job market in general. To the extent that the school emphasizes responding to the needs and interests of the child, awakening critical awareness, informal pedagogy, liberal discipline and flexible curricula, it will be conflicting, as we argued earlier, with employers' needs for recruits to the lower levels of the labour market equipped with basic yet flexible skills and appropriate attitudes, such as meticulousness and persistence in tasks (Neave, 1979).

It should be pointed out, however, that such had been the position of most teachers and pupils in secondary modern schools for many years without any very threatening changes in goals or practice having typically taken place. The difference here was that the movement away from external control was concerned with those mechanisms (public examinations) which regulate the first stages of entry to higher occupational status.

Thus ultimately, in the unlikely event of acceptance by universities, such a lack of external control over the form and content of certification could have posed a fundamental threat to traditional definitions of educational knowledge and standards. The student unrest of 1968 may well have produced an insecurity which, when exacerbated by an increasingly dismal economic picture at the beginning of the seventies and ensuing public concern over educational standards, resulted more or less directly in the institution of new, different means of control.

The new mechanisms of control being developed around the world, such as the English APU, can be seen as an ideal answer to the current need for 'kid-glove' control techniques. On the one hand, even the testing of a very small proportion of children when it is conducted on a national basis by those who hold the financial and bureaucratic power in the educational system — the DES (predictably to be emulated ere long by the local education authorities) — may well have a major impact on the educational system in allowing the State through the APU a new means of influencing educational content and standards. In this case it is conceivable that we shall soon witness a return to a more utilitarian emphasis in education and what Johnson (1976) has called, in the context of nineteenth-century English education, 'the cul-de-sac of skills' (see p. 51) — education geared to only basic competencies, the labour requirements of a technological society and the development of appropriate attitudes rather than free expression and personal development. On the other hand, external control of the content and practice of schooling in this form, rather than via a return to more formal controls through either a nationally imposed curriculum (as for example in France) or a resurgence of Mode I style external examinations based on externally-devised syllabuses, prevents a direct confrontation with the powerful lobby of liberal interest supporting school and teacher autonomy. Thus teacher-developed curricula and teacher-conducted Mode III assessment, progressive teaching methods and even the greater pupil and parent involvement heralded by the recent Taylor Report (1977) on school management, are rendered largely impotent as potential agents of educational 'liberation' (Holly, 1976) by these unobtrusive accountability controls. We are currently witnessing an international 'shortening of the reins' to guard against any tendency of the educational system to swing too far towards the expansion of opportunity, thereby subverting its equally crucial role in the process of social reproduction.

Summary and conclusions

This chapter has explored some recent international trends in assessment practices. Certainly, there is a good deal of evidence to support the identification of similar trends at this time in many industrialized countries towards a decline in formality in individual pupil assessment with a corresponding increase of other external forms of system control such as monitoring, standardized tests and centralized curricula. Equally though, it is important to stress that national education systems are each uniquely situated in an historical and contemporary social context which determines not only their position at a particular point of the continuum we identified in figure 1, but determines too the particular assessment techniques chosen at any particular time. Thus it cannot be argued that there is any unilateral trend. Rather a concept of oscillation is perhaps more helpful which situates the actual practices of assessment at any one time within the constant parameters of the functions of school assessment in an era of mass education. It is these same constants which are the continuing themes of this book. That assessment mechanisms develop to operate as a series of checks and balances on the education system in order to ensure its major function of perpetuating the social, economic and political *status quo*. That apparent changes in assessment procedures in recent years have been only superficial changes in response to changing educational ideals. That these changes have come about to defuse potential conflict and frustration whilst at the same time enabling schools to continue their traditional role of selecting and channelling pupils to different levels of the occupational and social hierarchy — a role which is indeed increasingly becoming problematic in a situation of chronic and large-scale youth unemployment. We have begun to explore too how assessment mechanisms are used to control the form and content of schooling, ensuring the preparation of youngsters in the necessary skills and attitudes for their various roles in advanced technological societies. Thus we have taken the analysis of chapter 1 a stage further in positing not only that the question of 'who', 'what', 'when' and 'how' are subservient to 'why', but also, that the answer to 'why' is a constant. We must now explore this argument in more detail by examining the complex relationship between school and society as mediated by the various assessment mechanisms in terms of more general theories of social reproduction and social control. This will be our concern in chapter 4.

4

Assessment
and ideology

Up to this point, I have principally been concerned to *identify* the origins and development of various assessment practices in their social context. The perspicacious reader will have already noted hints suggesting that any attempt to go beyond the mere *documentation* of changes in assessment practice towards an *explanation* of such changes, will be subject to the fundamental contradictions in perspective which characterize the contemporary sociology of education itself. In this chapter, my aim will be to explore the social functions of assessment at a more theoretical level in the light of such contrasting perspectives on the relationship between schooling and society.

The major dichotomy must be between explanations of educational assessment couched in a structural-functionalist, consensus view of society and those informed by a model of social conflict and control. Both views recognize the important role of education as an agency of both primary and secondary socialization, in the identification and preparation of youngsters for particular slots in the occupational hierarchy. There is, however, a fundamental difference between these two perspectives on assessment — a difference embedded in their more general identification of the role of schooling in society. That is to say, whether they see the education system operating in a rational and just way for the benefit of society as a whole or whether it is regarded as an instrument of repression in which the 'organization, method and content [of education] are designed to reproduce an existing social order and its necessary social and economic relationships' (Williams, 1977).

The prevailing ideology which has underlain both the birth and development of mass schooling may be characterized as 'liberal reformist'. In this view, education is seen as a process of social liberation and an avenue towards the creation of a more just, egalitarian society. The concept of the meritocracy is central for it is envisaged that the goals of education are rationally defined for the benefit of society as a whole and that those who have, by their own efforts and innate ability, made most progress towards these goals (as measured by various forms of assessment, notably public examinations), deserve to achieve the more desirable slots in the inevitable and necessary occupational and social hierarchy. The notion that all participants have an equal chance in the race is crucial to this perspective, both ideologically and in practical terms of making the maximum use of available talent. Thus, in this view, the impetus behind any educational reform is ostensibly the desire to approach more closely in educational provision the ideal of the meritocracy and of fair and efficient selection.

Many sociologists of education have been turning away from this Durkheimian-inspired, functionalist view in recent years, as the inequalities in educational achievement, despite more and more subtle explanations, consistently fail to respond to initiatives of reform such as 'comprehensive' and 'compensatory' education. They posit an alternative conflict perspective, in which the explanation of such failures is couched in terms of the desire of the dominant class to reproduce itself whilst, at the same time, stifling discontent and maintaining social order and control. Hence, assessment mechanisms cannot then be seen as objective arbiters of 'merit' but rather must be regarded, in the light of such theories, as subtle and complex agencies of social reproduction and control.

Such a distinction, although inevitably somewhat crudely identified in the space available here, is perhaps over-dichotomous for our purposes, for, once again, we confront the dilemma identified in chapter 1 between the liberation and control aspects of schooling, in which it is possible to justify elements of both perspectives in the operation of assessment procedures. It is arguable that even existing assessment mechanisms do allow a more open and rational allocation of occupational roles than was possible in the past before the era of mass schooling. Yet despite this apparent openness, the impact of class differentials in, for example, university entrance, seems to remain remarkably constant.

Both consensus and conflict theories of social reproduction have in many cases been criticized too for being over-structuralist and deterministic in an analysis which allows no autonomy to the education system as a result of the creative interpretations of the actors engaged in it. Even a cursory glance at contemporary schools must reveal the idiosyncratic nature of each school and even each classroom resulting from the impact of the unique reality of each actor involved on the process of interaction being negotiated in that social setting. An equally cursory glance will reveal a great deal of conflict in schools which belies any argument that the process of social reproduction works in the smooth, unproblematic way many macro-structural theories — consensual or conflict — would have us believe. This interactive perspective on assessment processes will be our concern in chapter 5 and with this important aside we may turn to the major concern of this chapter, which is a consideration of assessment practices in the light of various theories of the role of education in social reproduction. As a first step we must examine in a little more detail the nature of the ideology underpinning the contemporary practice of educational assessment.

An exercise in double-think

We know that, today, education in most parts of the world is dominated by a meritocracy ideal such as that described in chapter 2 which we saw emerging in England in the late nineteenth century. The extreme form of this ideology was clearly expressed in the English 1944 Education Act. This Act sought to provide an education system which would allow the individual to develop his abilities — whatever they were — to the maximum, thereby, too, enabling the society to make the best use of its 'pool of ability' in fulfilling its requirements for skilled manpower. Innate ability and personal effort were thought to be the only requirements for success. Assessment was of course in this view, an essential part of the necessary process of identification, allocation and attestation. Burton Clark (1962), as quoted by Karabel and Halsey (1977), provides us with a classic statement of this position:

> The existence of children of diverse ability *calls forth* the comprehensive school or the multi-school comprehensive structure, within which some students receive a broad general education but others take primarily a technical or commercial training. In short, increased quantity means greater vocationalism.... Sorting must take place at some point in the education structure. If at that level, it does not take place at the door, it must occur inside the doors, in the classroom and counselling office.

Although sociological researches of the 1950s demonstrated clearly the myth of 'equality of opportunity' and the extent of class bias in educational achievement, these findings resulted in the 'reformist' strategies typified in this country by comprehensivization, the raising of the school-leaving age and curriculum reform, rather than any radical questioning of the ethos of the education system itself. Assessment mechanisms in particular, the key to the operation of the education system as a sorting process for the allocation of occupational roles and thus an essential aspect of the meritocracy, went unquestioned at any fundamental level. Although as a result of research the intelligence test has had to forsake the central role it acquired when it emerged so conveniently to meet the need for apparently infallible identification of ability at the height of the meritocracy movement, its legacy still dominates the ideology of assessment. In particular it has been influential in confining the parameters of debate about assessment within largely technical boundaries so that assumptions about 'able' and 'less able' pupils, the content of assessment, the possibility of so-called 'objective' tests, and indeed a whole host of questions about, for example, the social functions of assessment of the type raised in this book, have been effectively obscured. The prevailing ideology of assessment is such that its central tenets are not seen as problematic (Broadfoot, 1978a). That it is both necessary and desirable for teachers and external examiners (but seldom the pupils themselves) to grade pupils according to certain kinds of performance (usually academic), in particular groupings of knowledge (some of higher status than others), usually in some kind of rank order, and on that basis to select some for opportunities leading to prestigious positions and usually high material rewards, and to reject others (i.e. the majority) for occupational roles of little reward and influence, is largely taken for granted by both experts and the general public.

However, an enormous number of research studies since the seminal work of Hartog and Rhodes in 1935 have demonstrated the fallibility and bias of the various types of assessment practice currently in use, particularly the most prestigious and widely-used essay-type examination. (See for example, Pidgeon and Yates, 1968; Lauwerys and Scanlon 1969; Ingenkamp, 1977.)

Many more writers have deplored the undesirable constraints on curriculum and pedagogy which result from assessment practices and describe the battle between educational ideals and the forces of pragmatism in terms that fall little short of Milton's *Paradise Lost*. Such criticisms are at least as old as the examination system itself and may be found in many of the major Government reports on education this century, such as that of Spens and Norwood, as well as individual protests (see, for example, Holmes, 1911; Schools Council, 1975; Lister, 1974; Stones, 1975; Kelly, 1971).

Yet, if anything, the legitimacy of formal assessment procedures is greater now than ever before, with the emphasis on testing, which emerged as part of our own 'Great Debate', being rehearsed in countries as ideologically and geographically far apart as the United States and China (Rogers, 1978; Gardner, 1978). Thus in 1977, Ingenkamp, in reviewing the evidence from both Europe and the United States, was able to write:

By 1970 a stage had been reached when traditional oral and written school examinations had been shown to be neither objective nor reliable; their content validity was jeopardised by subjective influence, predictive validity was low and the marking of different examiners could not be compared... (p. 14).

Thus it is perfectly possible that we are selecting our students by means of procedures that have no predictive value for academic success and that an examination is being used to determine academic success that has no predictive value for professional success ... we have not yet been able to produce research findings to refute the suspicion that we are continually selecting the wrong people with the wrong methods (p. 62).

Perhaps the most important point to emerge from this apparent anomaly whereby seemingly inefficient assessment practices continue to enjoy widespread support is that ideology, especially if it has a political function, does not necessarily have any relationship with empirical evidence. Indeed it may well ignore it or use it arbitrarily. As Kuhn (1970) points out, scientists throughout history have tended to 'adjust' pet theories rather than reject them when new evidence threatens, since evidence is rarely sufficiently conclusive — especially in the social sciences — to make rejection of a theory unavoidable. Thus the 'liberal reformist' tradition would explain the apparent disfunctions in assessment as inadequacies of technique, the solution to which is a pragmatic one of finding more accurate and thus more just means of performing the essential allocative functions of the educational system. That the education system may have evolved deliberately, if unconsciously, to favour a particular social group so that even with the most refined assessment techniques, no meritocracy is possible, makes assumptions about the nature of society that cannot be sustained in the 'liberal reformist' ideology and thus cannot be part of the explanation for the apparent anomalies in assessment procedures for those who adopt this ideology.

Rather, in this perspective, assessment — with all its technical faults — is seen as part of the liberating process of education —

an important spur to both pupil and teacher continually to be seeking higher 'standards'.

By contrast, those adopting a conflict model of society would identify the strength of the assessment ideology, despite its demonstrated weaknesses, as arising from the vital role of assessment as one of the major legitimation mechanisms in the social reproduction process of education. In this view, assessment in its form and content is seen to be biased in favour of the dominant group. Its importance lies not so much in whether it is efficient or not for *selection*, since the essential processes of social reproduction take place in the more gradual and informal processes of classroom identification, but whether it is efficient in *disguising* the hidden biases of the system so that the system can appear to be fulfilling the meritocracy ideal: the pretence of fulfilling the ideal of equality of opportunity is important, it is argued, for maintaining commitment to the system and thus perpetuating it. These arguments will perhaps become clearer as we look at these contrasting perspectives in more detail.

The liberal-reformist ideology

The expansion of formal schooling which has characterized the post-industrial revolution societies can be seen to go hand in hand with the ever-increasing demand for a more highly-skilled labour force. Or, as Karabel and Halsey (1977) put it, 'the expansion and the increasing differentiation of the educational system were inevitable outcomes of technologically determined changes in the occupational structure requiring ever more intricate skills'. It is significant that Durkheim's analysis of the shift from mechanical to organic solidarity and Tönnies' identification of the transition from the *Gemeinschaft* (community) to *Gesellschaft* (association), were almost contemporaneous with the massive expansion of State provision for education. That education had come to be seen as a vital part of industrial investment was only one aspect of the more general changes taking place in the social structure as both cause and effect of the expansion of formal schooling. Put another way, the creation of new and diverse opportunities, the breaking down of many of the hitherto insuperable barriers to social advancement, required new 'achievement'– rather than 'ascription'–oriented role allocation mechanisms. In Durkheim's view, to ensure the continuing equilibrium of society, such allocative mechanisms must be able to perform two crucial social functions. Firstly, there had to be found a way of allocating individuals to the various slots in the division of labour which would ensure that people were allocated roles in which they could make the best use of their skills and abilities. Secondly, the means of allocation must also ensure that those allocated to less desirable roles accepted the result as fair, if social control were to be maintained and an army of dissatisfied people prevented. 'The school has two tasks', writes Robinson (1977), 'within its integrative function, first to select out those most fitted for the elite slots in the beehive, and second, to convince the rest that the chosen are indeed born to rule.' Both structural-functionalist and conflict theory share this identification of the twofold function of assessment, differing only at the level of whether such functions are *indeed* in the best interest of all of those subjected to them, that is to say, society as a whole, rather than a particular group. Thus in functionalist theory, those who have demonstrated themselves to be most deserving and talented in relation to the central value system, will form the elite and the rest come to accept the more humble place that is all their own talent warrants. By contrast, conflict theory must define the twofold identification and control functions of educational assessment as the product of unequal power relationships between social groups, resulting in practices which for many must be essentially unjust, coercive, arbitrary and exploitative.

The drive for educational 'efficiency' through the maximum use of 'the pool of ability', the creation of opportunity for the deserving and the development of infallible techniques of identifying the said 'deserving', fitted extraordinarily well with the traditional socialist critique of inequality of educational opportunity between social classes. It is a testament to the pervasiveness of the meritocracy ideal that the Labour movement, rather than pursuing a specifically socialist education grounded in the cultural and educational traditions already existing in working-class communities, lent its support to the expansion of opportunity within the existing educational system. In the 1920s R.H.

91

Tawney's concern to expand secondary education from being the privilege of a few to the right of everyone was typical of the almost total preoccupation of the Labour movement with *access* to schooling at the expense of any concern about the *content* and *aims* of the education. Not only were there fears then, as now, about the dangers of creating an educational ghetto for the working class, belief in the feasibility and justice of a meritocracy was such that the need for educational reform was readily defined simply in organizational terms as the need for an expansion of opportunity to allow both the pursuit of individual justice and national efficiency (Finn *et al.*, 1977). It is not hard to see then why assessment too came to be seen as problematic only in relation to its efficiency; that it was a good thing, in facilitating the burgeoning meritocracy, was taken very much for granted.

Despite the dents created by sociologists in the last decade or two in this vision of a ladder of opportunity and, more recently, by the apparent failure of education to overcome environmental disadvantages; despite, too, the all too evident confrontations between increasingly entrenched radicals and progressives on the one hand and traditionalists concerned about 'standards' on the other, there appears to be little public questioning of what Bellaby (1977) has called the 'technological functionalism' model. School assessment maintains its dominant role in the allocation of career opportunities, so much so that the justification for this role rarely enters the field of debate. Indeed it is hard to imagine an alternative mechanism that would not be even more unjust. Writers such as Kamin (1974) have demonstrated how intelligence tests in particular have always worked so well that the mass of research devoted to refining and developing them rather than to any fundamental questioning of them, has served to reinforce the legitimacy of the dominant 'efficiency' model. However, as Hall (1977) points out, the dominant position of the liberal ideology, 'combined with its a-historical view of itself and the apparently universal consent it won for itself for a time, is indeed exactly what allows us to situate it as a historically-specific ideological formation'; an ideology which indeed may have served a very different purpose than that which it ostensibly supported. This brings us to our alternative explanation of the legitimation of contemporary assessment practices.

Assessment in a conflict perspective

Robinson (1977) criticizes the progressive liberal position in education for concentrating on the technical relations of production and ignoring the social and economic relations of authority and control integral to both production and schooling in a capitalist society. Equally, any analysis of the functions of educational assessment which stops short at its overt, technical role without taking into account its vital, if more covert role, as a manifestation of power and control, is also seriously inadequate. Hextall and Sarup (1977) refer to McHugh *et al.*'s (1974) distinction between evaluation based on power which is imposed by force and evaluation which is apparently rational or scientific, making reference to the standards of what constitutes knowledge in the community as a whole. Hextall and Sarup (1977) and Hextall (1976) refute this claim for 'scientific' evaluation, arguing that all school assessment involves the implicit acceptance of a particular set of standards and values embedded in a particular economic structure and political order. Thus, they argue, it can never be a technical act alone but is essentially a political act.

> Evaluation implies and refers to the giving of 'acceptable' reasons grounded upon implicit or explicit notions of 'standards'. (What constitute 'good' reasons and rules, their negotiation and legitimation are important questions.) (Hextall and Sarup, 1977)

If we see the apparently objective endorsement of assessment as essentially a political act, this raises a host of new issues. The consensus model of society (and hence the education system) working equally in the interests of all rather than particular interest group(s) — the ideology which underpins the liberal reformist tradition — is brought into question. The form and content of assessment takes on a new significance as a reflection of class differences in the production and communication of knowledge and understanding. The complementary operation of the hidden curriculum — all those aspects of school life not part of formal teaching but highly instrumental in socializing pupils into appropriate attitudes and modes of behaviour — and the host of similarly informal and covert assessment practices, may likewise be the subject of different kinds of question.

There is a growing body of evidence (see for example, Halsey, 1978; Tyler, 1977) that the ever expanding educational opportunities have done little to erode class differentials in educational achievement. Many sociologists have sought to account for this phenomenon by adopting a perspective in which education is seen as a means of social reproduction rather than social mobility. Although such conflict theories cover a wide range of both Marxist and non-Marxist perspectives, they share a common emphasis on the need to understand society in terms of class conflict and control by a dominant group, which will seek to perpetuate and legitimate its privileged position. Typically, education is seen as a key mechanism for this reproduction and legitimation. For the sake of clarity, I have chosen to confine the discussion of the role of educational assessment in such a conflict perspective to three of the most influential and relevant theories.

The correspondence theory

The leading exponents of this theory are the American economists Bowles and Gintis in *Schooling in Capitalist America* (1976). Their ideas emphasize the important correspondence between the social relations of capitalist production and the social relations of the school. From a neo-Marxist perspective, they see assessment in a broad spectrum comprising five important sets of pupil/worker characteristics. One of these five sets of characteristics assessed is that traditionally emphasized in assessment procedures of cognitive achievement, which in this case includes both scholastic achievement and concrete technical and operational skills such as typewriting. More important though are the second set — behavioural characteristics such as motivation, perseverance and co-operation. The third set of characteristics for assessment relates not to the performance of a particular task, but concerns 'modes of self-presentation' in speech, dress or self-perception. These 'modes of presentation', Bowles and Gintis argue, play a vital role as *legitimators* of differences in the occupational hierarchy, as do the fourth and fifth sets of criteria — ascriptive characteristics such as race, sex and age, and credentials (other relevant differentiators between individuals, such as the level and prestige of schooling). From their statistical analysis of the various factors influencing economic success they conclude that 'a family's position in the [United States] class structure is reproduced primarily by mechanisms operating independently of the inheritance, production and certification of intellectual skills' (Bowles and Gintis, 1976). In other words, whilst overtly emphasizing objective academic assessment, schools are in fact assessing pupils on a wide range of other criteria, which are either ascriptive and thus not open to pupils to change, or highly subjective. The fact that these assessments strongly influence the expectations teachers have of pupils and hence their subsequent interaction with them, compounds the assessment by encouraging the pupil to build up a particular self-image. This highly significant aspect of assessment we shall discuss in detail in chapter 5.

The importance of the emphasis on apparently objective tests and on intelligence tests in particular in this perspective is, as has already been argued, in reinforcing the authoritarian, hierarchical, stratified and unequal economic system of production and in reconciling the individual to his place in it so that he comes to see such a system as natural (i.e. adopts a liberal reformist ideology!). Thus Bowles and Gintis would explain the apparent failure of massive compensatory education programmes in the United States such as Project Headstart and Follow Through, Project Talent and, by implication, in Britain the Education Priority Areas (Halsey, 1972) and the continuing discrepancy between the achievements of the various social classes, as being a necessary reflection of the inequalities inherent in capitalist production. Although sociologists of very different perspectives have been largely agreed on the important differential effects of family socialization patterns on school achievement, Bowles and Gintis stress that these differing self-perceptions, aspirations and behavioural characteristics are not eroded by the school — as compensatory education programmes have sought to do — but are rather *compounded* in school as staff categorize pupils according to a wide range of criteria drawn from each of the five sets of assessment characteristics outlined above.

Crucial to their argument, too, however, is that the rationale for selection and allocation at school, its organization on bureaucratic and hierarchical lines, with stratification based on ability, age and sex and rewards in the form of marks and promotion, corresponds exactly with the norms of the work place. Dale (1977) puts the point neatly: 'This process of sorting, shifting and positioning prepares pupils for being sorted, shifted and positioned in world society, a process which it both anticipates and legitimates through the frequently mutually reinforcing cognitive and behavioural criteria involved.' In this sense then, assessment can be seen not only as an instrumental mechanism, but as a vital part of the socialization process which trains pupils to accept external judgement, external rewards and external control. John Holt (1969), with his usual pungency, describes the process by which, as some of their first lessons in school, children learn to work for external rewards alone, so that gradually they become as alienated from their school work as any factory worker. 'In school he learns like every buck private or conscript labourer . . . how not to work when the boss isn't looking, how to know when he is looking, how to make him think you are working when you know he is looking.'

It is significant, in this context, that assessment is almost exclusively regarded as an individual activity in the same way that wages are an individual return for work done, teaching pupils early the ethics of individualism and competition, also intrinsic both to capitalist society and hence to education, as Durkheim (1969) has argued. Indeed so fundamental is this relationship to school life as we know it that it is difficult not to endorse Hextall's (1976) sentiments: 'the pain and mystery of this for me is that such a fundamentally quantitative, calculative orientation to work is so embedded that an alternative version is literally inconceivable.' And herein lies the key to the 'correspondence' principle. Bowles and Gintis argue that the division of labour is not, as is popularly supposed, the most technically efficient, productive form of organizing labour. Rather, they assert, it is essential to the maintenance of an alienated work force divided amongst itself which is then far too demoralized to foster any serious criticisms of the *status quo*. So in schools, it may be argued, assessment is important for dividing pupils amongst themselves and thus for diffusing any possibility of a concerted attack on the existing model of schooling.

Certainly there is plenty of evidence (e.g. Becher and Maclure, 1978; SED, 1977) which demonstrates the tight control formal assessment procedures keep on innovation in schools. Open, progressive primary practices are quickly sacrificed for the 'real work' of the secondary school (Kogan, 1978). Many secondary teachers readily admit their impotence to bring about change or even fulfil their own educational ideals in the face of the exigencies of the exam syllabus and its individualist orientation (Raven, 1977). Even at the higher education level, student radicalism must be largely defenceless in the face of the powerful interests behind the final examination.

Assessment as a mechanism of social reproduction

The insights of Bourdieu and his colleagues of the Centre de Sociologie Européenne in Paris are in many ways complementary to those of Bowles and Gintis in providing an understanding of the social functions of educational assessment from a conflict perspective. In particular the common emphasis on the central role of non-cognitive assessment is significant. However in this case it is the class bias of the apparently objective, formal assessment procedures themselves which are seen as especially significant. Bourdieu's notion of 'cultural capital' embodies a conception of schooling in which, rather than corresponding to and being determined by the social relations of production, the organization is specifically designed to favour those with elite cultural backgrounds. The elite, finding themselves no longer able to perpetuate their privileged status simply by financial capital, have, according to Bourdieu, organized teaching and in particular, selection procedures, to favour those with culturally-specific skills. Thus lack of achievement by particular social groups comes to be understood as a product of differential socialization, especially class variations in self-perceptions and aspirations. Although very similar to Bowles and Gintis in this emphasis on the operation of non-cognitive characteristics in assessment, there is a crucial difference between the two theories in that Bourdieu's work stresses the cultural bias even of apparently objective cognitive assessment procedures as well as the differential effect of class on aspirations and the ability to respond to teaching.

Bourdieu identifies a twofold discrimination on the basis of social class. First there are the social disadvantages which mean that children from the 'lower' classes — who overall achieve a lower success rate anyway — must be *more* successful for their family and teachers to consider encouraging further study. This means, according to Bourdieu (1974), that although educational achievement and entry to selective institutions depends closely on social class, overall inequality of entry depends more on the inequality of those of equal attainment who actually *enter* such institutions than an inequality of attainment as such. Such inequalities, argues Bourdieu, are compounded by the possession or lack, according to social class, of 'cultural capital' — a set of attitudes and behavioural characteristics which match the aristocratic culture of the school. The 'style, taste and wit', the 'correct dress and bearing, accent and style of speech of the elite' which is natural to a particular class become the yardstick against which *all* are judged. Thus for example, Bourdieu and Passeron (1976) analyse how conventional modes of assessment in France such as the essay, the interview and the oral examination (very widely used in France), are geared to the literary and linguistic tradition of elite French culture. Goody and Watt (1962) echo this point in their more general identifications of literacy skills as one of the major axes of differentiation in industrial societies. They further make the point that such emphasis on reading and writing is another way of stressing the individualistic aspect of assessment discussed earlier, since such activities are essentially solitary.

Assessment as part of the hegemony

Further insights into the functioning of assessment as a mechanism of class reproduction are to be found in the Marxian concept of hegemony. As defined by Gramsci this refers to the legitimation of the prevailing social order by the unity of a particular set of political, social and economic forces which saturates the society to such an extent that it produces among its members an unquestioning common-sense understanding of the existing order as the *natural* order (Williams, 1976). Thus it is possible to conceive the whole rationale for school assessment — the ethos of motivation, selection, attestation and even accountability, as encapsulating the particular set of social, political and economic conditions prevalent in capitalist society. That education should be concerned to teach many things likely to be of little use in later life; that it should be conducted in hierarchical and bureaucratic institutions in which the pupil is relatively powerless; that it should foster competitiveness at a personal, institutional and even national level; that pupils should have almost no say in what they are taught and above all that allocation to differential social positions should take place largely on the basis of demonstrably inaccurate assessment mechanisms, may all be attributed to the prevailing hegemony which prevents genuinely alternative conceptions of education, even if conceived (e.g. Freire, 1971, 1972; Illich, 1971), from entering into any serious arena of debate (Broadfoot, 1978b).

There are echoes here of Bourdieu's complex concepts of 'symbolic violence' and the 'cultural arbitrary' which are, he argues, the means by which the elite succeed in imposing their cultural meanings — the rationale that underlies their whole way of life and through which they achieve and maintain their superior status — on the potentially conflicting cultural meanings produced through the social interaction of those in a very different relationship to the means of production.

There are echoes too of Williams' (1976) identification of the complementarity of the Marxian concepts of base and superstructure — the one the relations of production, the real social existence of man, the other the ideology ratifying the domination of a particular class and expressed in a wide variety of legal, social, political, religious and possibly even artistic activity and institutions.

All these theories though, are much more complex than the mere positing of a model in which the elite — as in some kind of conspiracy theory — sets the rules of the game to its own advantage and at the same time finds ways to convince the population as a whole that these rules are objective and fair. Rather the process of class domination must be understood in the way that the ideology underpinning the economic domination of the elite so transforms and pervades society that it can neither be recognized or distinguished as anything more than common sense. The domination of meritocratic thinking in Western industrial society is a classic example.

There are obvious connections — here too with 'new directions' perspectives in the sociology of education as expressed for example in Young (1971). Here Young stresses the importance of regarding the commonly used forms of knowledge and, by implication, assessment, as products of a particular set of social power relationships — or, to use the Marxian term — of the hegemony. So much of the taken for granted parameters of education — terms such as teacher, pupil or examination, hierarchical relationships of learning between teacher and taught, differences in status between subjects such as Latin and home economics — cease to have meaning, Young argues, except as the manifestation of elite culture as it effectively dominates even our ability to conceive of alternative categories of knowledge or organization.

Assessment and control: a new perspective

It is difficult in the space of a few pages to situate assessment in the context of highly complex and controversial theories currently emerging in the sociology of education and not cause a certain amount of indigestion. This chapter will have succeeded if it only convinces the reader that the 'how', 'what', 'who', and 'when' questions with which we started this book are essentially political and not technical questions alone, as so much of the literature seems to imply (e.g. McIntosh, 1974; Rowntree, 1977). As Williams (1977) asserts, 'all the orthodox propositions and research findings about selection procedures, examinations and teaching methods are necessarily transvalued'.... Although there are major differences between the three conflict theories that have been discussed in this chapter, there are equally large areas of agreement. Each requires a consideration of assessment mechanisms as important instruments in the reproduction of *inequality* rather than as the tollgates to equality. Each requires that the form and/or the content of assessment be identified as biased towards the social and cultural traditions of the dominant social groups whilst operating as key agencies of control by legitimating such bias under the guise of objectivity. There is a common emphasis on legitimation which, as expressed in the dominant ideology of assessment as we know it, is so effective as to allow such assessment to be seen as an essential aspect of the educational process, and to keep it from even entering the arena of educational debate. Thus Bowles and Gintis (1977) argue the general case in stressing the inadequacy of regarding assessment purely in terms of its visible, cognitive forms, for it cannot be divorced from the total perspective, 'in which social, racial, ethnic and sexual differentiation and differential patterns of socialization interact with the hierarchical division of labour ... in addition to performance-related individual capacities normally developed on a class basis, [for] beneath the surface of rationality, meritocracy and performance-oriented efficiency, the capitalist economic system operates a subtle network of ascriptions and symbolic differentiations quite as well articulated as the most complex caste system.'

In the insights of conflict theory lies an explanation for the repeated failure of educational innovations informed by the liberal reformist ideology. The expansion of opportunity and the apparent institution of a meritocracy ignores the important processes of social reproduction operating via the hidden curriculum in which pupils' differing self-perceptions, socialization experiences and class-based competencies determine how they respond to the three message-systems of the school — curriculum, pedagogy and evaluation (Bernstein, 1977). As a result, it may be argued, pupils come to see themselves as legitimately allocated to a particular point in the occupational hierarchy and come to develop the appropriate social attributes for such roles.

In touching on such processual aspects of social allocation we deliberately trespass on the territory of the next chapter in order to bridge the essentially arbitrary division between structure and process and link the macro-perspective of the relationship between education and the occupational structure with which we have been concerned in this chapter, and the 'micro'-insights of how this relationship is realized at the level of the individual classroom, to which we now turn. Since, as Sharp and Green (1975) point out, it is not possible either to explain social interaction adequately, devoid of the symbolic context determined by the macro-structure of society, or to draw up an adequate paradigm for the social structural relationships of society which cannot be discovered in its processual aspects at the level of individual interaction, the analysis of the operation of assessment mechanisms in the classroom itself presented in the next chapter must be seen as an extension and substantiation of the issues raised in this.

Summary

This chapter has attempted to explore the frequently ignored area of the ideology underlying school assessment as we know it. The justification for assessment offered in the liberal reformist tradition of education is contrasted with some of the more recent explanations offered as part of the analysis of schooling as an agency of social reproduction. Rejecting a once popularly held belief that existing forms of school assessment provide for a meritocracy by being objective and relevant, thereby freeing selection from the operation of prejudice, nepotism and various other ascribed criteria, the insights of conflict theory argue an important role for assessment in reinforcing elite culture in three ways. Firstly, it is argued, assessment covers a much broader range of socially-differentiating characteristics than is commonly supposed. Secondly, the content and method of the assessment relate to the culturally produced meanings and skills of the elite, thereby enabling the elite to reproduce their position more easily. Thirdly, the importance of assessment in obscuring such class bias in education through its apparent objectivity, and hence of legitimating the system in the eyes of *all* its participants, is emphasized. Little attempt is made to reconcile these two perspectives, the aim being rather to shift the focus of debate about assessment practices to a more profound level.

5

Assessment in the classroom

Those who have forgotten the agonies and the ecstasies of the classroom might be forgiven, if they have read this far, for forming the impression that school assessment is a periodic activity, surrounded at particular times with a great deal of brouhaha and that it exists to provide for formal selection at various stages of schooling and to keep schools up to scratch. Those for whom the realities of classroom life still daily impinge will readily reject this view in realizing how much assessment is part of the everyday experience of both teachers and pupils. In chapter 1 I argued that all forms of assessment reflect a similar set of values and share a common set of assumptions and functions. This chapter will attempt to substantiate this assertion by identifying the various forms of informal classroom assessment and examining their effects.

Cognitive tests

The most obvious aspects of classroom assessment are the tests that take place as part of the ongoing teaching and learning process. The teacher will set tests in order to diagnose strengths and weaknesses of individual pupils, to gauge the progress of the class as a whole and to consolidate learning. From time to time, especially in the primary school, he or she may administer 'standardized' tests in order to judge the progress of the pupils against some wider standards than that of his or her own class alone. In all such testing activities, the teacher probably feels he or she is getting an objective picture of the knowledge and skills of the pupils concerned. Indeed such a belief is central to the organization of our schools in terms of setting, streaming and reporting. Research, however, has revealed the highly subjective and indeed biased operation of many such assessments both in content and technique.

Firstly, the testing situation is an interactive situation between tester and tested. It can therefore not be seen as a neutral process but as subject to the same interpretation and negotiation that inheres in any social interaction. As Erickson (1970) points out, all experience is relative and thus all interpretation — of questions, of appropriate answers— must be equally relative. A class of thirty children given a 'standardized' test are making thirty individual responses to it. These responses, similar to the extent that the test relates to experiences the pupils have shared, such as teaching, are nevertheless uniquely influenced in each case by all sorts of personal characteristics. Application to the test, for example, depends upon a whole host of individual influences such as home background, previous school experience, attitude towards the tester and so on. Roth (1974) has shown for example that the ethnic group of the tester may well influence the pupil's responses to a test. Feeling anxious or threatened may affect a pupil's ability to recall knowledge at a particular time; he may have the required knowledge but be unable to reproduce it in the form required. Cicourel (1974) criticizes such tests for typically only being concerned to measure the *products* of learning as demonstrated in a few highly restricted ways. By so doing, he argues, the tests fail to monitor the equally important cognitive *processes* involved in the testing situation and in particular, the way these processes are affected by their interactive setting. He argues that the entire nature/

nurture controversy on the determination of intelligence which raged for half a century, totally ignored the profound impact on test scores made by the interactive situation in which the test inevitably takes place. Even if the test is administered by machine, the situation is still a social one in that the *making* and *interpretation* of the tests are social acts — they embody value judgements emanating from the dominant culture as to what constitutes evidence of 'intelligence' and what constitutes valid realization of 'educational knowledge'. That particular types of verbal skills dominate testing as much as they do teaching (Bernstein, 1971) ensures an advantage to those children who come from (usually middle-class) homes where they are encouraged to develop such skills. As we saw in chapter 4, many sociologists have argued that this is indeed an essential aspect of the reproductive and legitimating function of the school. Mackay (1974) puts the point with some force:

> I would suggest that the powerful pronouncement of science sanctifies common-sense prejudice and legitimizes the production of persons whose qualifications (or lack of them) block them from anything but menial or semi-skilled jobs. But it is a vicious circle since the objective test started from these prejudiced beliefs about the world. The tests are used by test constructors, teachers, administrators and politicians to support their own beliefs and value systems.... In *use* measures of performance relative to some unexplicated standard (usually face validity, i.e. constructor's common-sense view of the world) become an objective measure of competence that have a determinative impact on students' lives ... hanging on this thin thread is the entire occupational and status structure of society.

Thus, Roth (1974) argues, all sorts of 'intelligence' are not measured in tests and thus 'intelligence' is a social phenomenon rather than the individual phenomenon it has usually been claimed to be.

Not only does the test tell the teacher something about the pupil, it usually tells the pupil something about himself — information he may choose to accept or reject as irrelevant. Whatever his reaction, the possession of such information by both teacher and pupil irrevocably influences their future interaction. How the teacher sees and acts upon the information will depend on his or her expectations for that pupil built upon a range of background information, personal characteristics and previous similar tests. The result may be a confirmation of a growing stereotype of the pupil as 'less able' or 'bright' or, if it does not correspond to the teacher's expectation for that pupil, the evidence of this particular test may be rejected as an anomaly. Fleming and Anttonen's (1971) research led them to suggest that: 'Teachers assess children, reject discrepant information and operate on the basis of previously developed attitudes towards and knowledge about children and tests.'

Teachers' attitudes to and expectations of individual children will be expressed in their varying interactions with pupils so that individuals very quickly come to learn what the teacher thinks of them. How any one pupil reacts to this information will certainly be influenced by a host of factors including his perception of his own abilities, his aspirations and his attitude to the subject, the teacher and the school as a whole. To the extent that the pupil accepts a teacher's identification of him as 'able', 'dull', 'passive' or 'naughty' and acts accordingly, the initial identification will be reinforced and have a compounding effect on all subsequent interactions between that teacher and pupil. Typically too, as a result of both written and verbal reports, impressions will be passed on from teacher to teacher so that gradually stereotyped expectations of the pupil are built up.

This stereotype is likely to be reinforced again by the organizing categories of the school, in that when a child is allocated to a particular ability set or stream on the basis of the sort of evaluation I have been describing, such information about him as an individual will be seen in the context of the more general stereotype of the 'A' stream pupil or a 'non-certificate class' built up in the totality of previous interactions between teachers and pupils, teachers and teachers and pupils and pupils in the school. Thus not only will it become increasingly hard for the pupil to resist accepting and acting on the imputation of a particular identity, this identity will tend to be related to pre-existing stereotypes of pupil 'types' or what Sharp and Green (1975) refer to as 'reified typifications'. Teacher actions based

106

on such typifications may well ignore important characteristics of the pupil which lie outside the 'ideal type' definitions. We shall return to this crucial process of stereotype formation later in the chapter but first we must turn to the other major aspect of classroom assessment — non-cognitive assessment — as the two aspects of assessment — cognitive and non-cognitive — are inextricably interwoven and our separation of them is essentially arbitrary.

Non-cognitive assessment

When a pupil first goes to school, he soon learns that he must 'adapt to the continued and pervasive spirit of evaluation that will dominate his school years ... that tests are as indigenous to the school environment as are textbooks or pieces of chalk...' (Jackson, 1968). He learns that evaluations will be forthcoming from his teachers and his classmates and he learns to judge himself by their criteria. He may well be unaware, though, of how wide the range of the assessments being made of him are. Not only is the teacher concerned about academic progress, he or she will be even more concerned about behaviour and attitudes since establishing control is a necessary precondition for teaching. Parsons (1959) identifies two parameters of assessment used by the teacher to distinguish between children. The one, termed 'achievement', relates to learning skills and the acquisition of knowledge. The other, referred to as the 'moral' dimension by Parsons, includes non-cognitive attributes of behaviour and work-habits. From the initially fairly homogenous group of new entrants to the elementary school, the 'good' pupil, according to Parsons, is progressively more easy to distinguish by his achievement on *both* 'moral' and 'achievement' axes.

Empirical research has substantiated and elaborated Parsons' assertion that non-cognitive assessment is at least as important as the more obvious academic evaluations of the classroom. Greaney and Kellaghan (1972), for example, found that over 50 per cent of the variance in class placement was based on non-cognitive assessment, a proportion which was even higher for pupils identified as 'less academic'. In a study of the criteria

107

used informally by teachers for the assessment of pupils, Wood and Napthali (1975) identify six constructs, both cognitive and non-cognitive, on the basis of which teachers are likely, to a greater or lesser extent, to differentiate between pupils: the involvement of the pupil in the learning situation; the ability the pupil has in the subject; his overall ability; his behaviour; the quality and tidiness of the work presented and the interest displayed by the pupil in the subject. Indeed the impossibility of avoiding non-cognitive assessment is made clear in the comment of a teacher quoted in Hoste and Bloomfield (1975):

> We make no formal attempt to assess non-cognitive qualities but let me say in qualification of that, that all the points are inherent in the assessment because it's so subjective. You cannot assess a child whom you have taught for five terms and not have in your assessment some recognition of these qualities. It's impossible.

This seems to be an unusually perceptive comment by a teacher, for Brown and McIntyre (1977) show clearly that teachers' conscious preoccupation is almost exclusively with pupils' 'general ability' in making evaluations and that other characteristics they are aware of as affecting pupils' responses to their teaching, such as enthusiasm or disruptiveness, are rarely mentioned. Morrison (1974) too found no teacher in his study who recognized this non-cognitive element in assessment in setting out to test or assess overtly such characteristics.

Stereotype formation and the 'self-fulfilling prophecy'

It is the theme of this book that such apparent anomalies are not accidental but serve a social purpose. The fact that assessment in the classroom is invested with a mythology of objectivity and ostensibly confined to legitimate academic matters, whilst in fact it is highly subjective and comprehensive, is central to the school's operation as a mechanism of social allocation. Put simply, non-cognitive and ascriptive characteristics of pupils such as attitude to learning, self-control, accent, sex, ethnic and class background, allow teachers to categorize pupils almost as soon as they meet them and long before they have a chance to form a judgement of their intellectual ability. From past experience and indeed from sociological studies which may be said to have done a disservice in respect of reinforcing particular teacher expectations for identifiable social groups, teachers know that children from immigrant or low socio-economic background typically do less well at school than their 'nicely-spoken', attentive, mainly middle-class peers. In the debate about *why* this should be the case, the major contribution made by teachers' expectations was until recently overlooked. The more-or-less clearly defined expectations of teachers in relation to these various socially determined criteria influence the interaction of teacher and pupil from the outset so that, for example, children expected on the basis of non-academic criteria to do well have been shown actually to receive more encouragement from the teacher whilst the less promising child will receive less academic attention and more behavioural criticism (Good and Brophy, 1970; Silberman, 1969).

Sharp and Green (1975) provide us with several detailed case-studies of the process whereby an initial typification of a child on the basis of the teacher's impression of his or her home background and the child's behaviour on entering the reception class is compounded or, in rare cases, refuted. They cite the example of Karen— a girl from a family previously identified by the school as troublesome. The teacher's resultant predisposition to expect 'difficulties' with Karen are reinforced by the child's noisy and raucous behaviour on entering school. Sharp and Green analyse the results thus:

> The child was critically expected to show symptoms of (normal) deviance and the teacher treated it as naughty and ill-mannered. When it settled into a busy' role (i.e. desired behaviour) the teacher invoked neo-psychiatric categories and rationales for its avoidance of her and poor intellectual start.... The solution Karen had adopted to her identification by the teacher as 'loud' and 'naughty' was to withdraw from interaction with the teacher, to be shy and reticent in her company, and to spend most of her time playing at an activity which fitted the teacher's reality test for 'insecurity' and 'dullness'....

109

By contrast, Sharp and Green cite the example of Linda — who started with an equally adverse typification but who, because of her ability to fit into the teacher's system of relevancies very quickly and her willingness to respond to the teacher's authority, soon began to approximate much more closely to the teacher's identification of the 'ideal' pupil. The fact that Linda actually received more of the teacher's attention than usual as a result of her critical identification by the teacher as potentially difficult also gave Linda, argue Sharp and Green, more opportunity than other pupils to learn the underlying structure of rules and regulations on which success depends. It was Linda's willingness and ability to conform to these rules which was crucial in the changing of her identification from a 'potentially difficult' pupil to a 'very good' pupil.

As early as 1964 both Jackson and Douglas identified in their research an independent effect of self-fulfilling prophecy operating against working-class children and in favour of middle-class children. Nash (1976) provides a telling illustration of this effect in quoting a study by Rist (1970) of a first year *nursery* school class. The pupils were streamed after only eight days in the school. This streaming took place on the basis of the only information readily available to the teacher — that pertaining to the child's background and the teacher's own expectations based on characteristics such as dress, accent and social skills. The teacher expressed these initially conceived differential expectations in the allocation of both academic and social tasks, such as being class monitor. This quickly established a status hierarchy between the pupils. If, as has been argued, pupils perform in response to teachers' expectations and their own self-concept progressively produced through interaction influenced by such expectations, then it is not surprising that in Rist's study, the scores on the ('objective') reading test at the end of the year reflected the initial streaming almost exactly! 'Teachers', writes Nash (1974) 'form an "ideal type" of what is necessary for success; allow subjective evaluations based on this to influence their educational judgement and regard the results of "objective" tests as somehow *independent* of their actions, indeed as justification for them.'

Keddie (1971) has explored this same process in action in the secondary school situation in her study of the different message systems operating in the 'A' and 'C' streams of a particular comprehensive school. She describes the process by which pupils, having been allocated to and thus labelled as belonging to a particular stream, are subject to differentiated teacher perceptions. She argues both that teachers came to 'know' pupils through their classification in a particular stream and that this 'knowledge' is based primarily on expectations of social-class linked behaviour from which imputations about intellectual ability are made. Thus the stereotypes of 'A'-nes and 'C'-ness cover both cognitive and non-cognitive attributes. As a result, argues Keddie, teachers use the complex category of 'ability' as expressed in streaming to differentiate their teaching in terms of high status, abstract knowledge for top streams and low status, practical knowledge for bottom streams. This in turn, according to Keddie, results in and perpetuates the existing discrepancies in society between high status individuals on the one hand, whose power emanates from their mastery of the dominant culture and, on the other, low status individuals who are powerless to do more than acquiesce in an alien culture since they are never given the opportunity to develop a critical consciousness. Brown and McIntyre (1977) argue a similar point in stressing that 'general ability', which in their study they found to account for as little as 15 per cent of variations in achievement in science, is nevertheless significant as the organizing category for the production of relatively permanent stereotypes which influence teachers' expectations and interactions.

A great deal of controversy has characterized the notion of the self-fulfilling prophecy since the first detailed study of its effects by Rosenthal and Jacobsen (1968) in which they claimed to have shown the independent effect of teacher expectation on pupil achievement. A large number of studies have offered both refutations and substantiations of Rosenthal and Jacobsen's findings. In the light of more recent studies of the process of stereottpe formation of the kind we have been discussing, there can now be little doubt of its significance.

This is not, of course, to argue that children do not enter school differentially equipped to succeed as a result of their social background. Bernstein (1970) and Bourdieu (1971) have

111

both shown clearly that in many ways, teachers are justified in expecting the middle-class child to be 'more able' since the entire ethos of the school, having its origins in elite culture, reflects that culture in its values, its curriculum, its pedagogy and its language. It is rather to argue that these existing social class differentials are *compounded* by the differential expectations teachers have of pupils as individuals, as classes and indeed from school to school, as Becker (1976) has shown in his study of the different expectations of pupils held by teachers in schools in 'good' and 'bad' areas of Chicago. Undoubtedly children are not a homogenous group in the teacher's eyes when they enter the classroom. Often they have been assessed even before arriving for their first day at school. As a result of visible social class characteristics which tend to be associated in the teacher's mind with expectations of 'ability', from their first entry to school, children, although inhabiting ostensibly the same classroom, are in fact in a number of very different social worlds.

There are some grounds too, for believing that 'assessment climates' vary from subject to subject so that for example Morrison (1974) found that teachers of English placed greater emphasis on informal, affective assessment in contrast to maths teachers who were more preoccupied with cognitive achievement. Thus it may well be the case that the differential curriculum emphasis between 'high' and 'low' ability groups which frequently results in 'less-able' pupils pursuing a more practically-oriented course of studies, is reflected in the provision of different emphases in assessment. The greater emphasis in practical subjects on social skills and affective objectives which Morrison identified may lead to a more subjective assessment upon which social class characteristics are likely to have an even larger effect than on more cognitive assessments. Obviously research would be needed to substantiate or refute this argument but it is conceivably the case that pupils who are most likely to be the receivers of negative non-cognitive evaluations by teachers are also those likely to be most subjected to them. Certainly Bourdieu and Passeron's (1976) research, which suggests that social class differentials are more likely to be prejudicial in the 'arts' than in the sciences, would seem to go some way to supporting the argument.

Assessment and the development of pupil subcultures

Thus assessment in the classroom is a dynamic cumulative process in which the expectations aroused in the teacher by his or her initial characterization of the pupil's home background are reinforced in the interaction of the classroom to compound failure or success. It has already been mentioned that a crucial factor in this process of reinforcement is the consolidation of pupil self-image as a result of classroom interaction. Davidson and Lang (1960) have shown how pupils can evaluate themselves very accurately according to the teacher's criteria. The evaluation of the pupil by the teacher is consolidated amongst the pupils themselves who, conditioned by the ethos of the school to accept the teacher's definitions as correct, are likely to adopt the teacher's stereotypes in their interaction with each other and thereby reinforce them. Hargreaves (1976) documents the process of interaction leading from perhaps a fairly casual remark by a teacher, the compounding of this possibly insignificant evaluation to the extent that the pupil and his peers accept it as legitimate and allow it to influence subsequent interaction, to the formation of a permanent 'label' or stereotype — 'disruptive', 'truant', 'swot' or even 'disturbed'.

The labelling process is yet more significant because as Jackson (1968) points out, 'all pupils learn to employ psychological buffers that protect them from some of the wear and tear of classroom life'. In particular the pupil constantly in receipt of negative evaluations which, as we have seen, the unidimensional value system of the school is likely to apply to his behaviour as well as his academic achievement, learns, for his own protection, to 'play it cool', to devalue these evaluations and develop an alternative value system in which he can experience success. These attempts to defend himself against the sense of failure meted out by the school will be enhanced to the extent that he can band together with other pupils in the same situation. Thus gradually, as teachers know only too well, recalcitrant cliques and infamous classes develop, characterized by a rejection of the school's values and frequently, the elevation of alternative values such as peer group comradeship or machismo (Woods, 1979). The terrors of the RSLA class or the bottom-

113

stream third year are thus common spectres in secondary schools. Lambart (1976) and Willis (1977), among others, have shown how these cliques are associated with 'ability' (as defined by the school) and social class, resulting in each group having its own attitudes towards work, school, and other pupils, as well as definitions of appropriate behaviour both in and out of the classroom. Hargreaves' (1967) classic study of the more formal peer groups occasioned by streaming illustrated clearly a distinction between the school-oriented values of the relatively high-achieving, high status 'A' stream and the anti-school 'delinquescent' values of the 'D' stream.

A processual account of the development of school subcultures from classroom evaluations goes a long way in accounting for the development of individual pupil careers. But it can only tell part of the story. Increasingly, the importance of studying interaction within the context of the wider socio-economic structure of society is being recognized by sociologists of the classroom. A blending of structural and processual analyses can provide a better understanding 'of the educational process, the interactions of both students and teachers, in terms of the organization of the societal division of labour, how the societal division of labour not only influences the individual success of the student but also affects variations in the forms of interaction which take place in schools' (Apple and Wexler, 1978). In so doing sociologists have begun to return to the example set so long ago by Durkheim in his *L'Evolution Pédagogique en France*, in which he stresses the importance of recognizing the constraints which larger patterns of power and control in the society place upon the process of schooling, and not least the definition, transmission and evaluation of school knowledge. Thus, although the recent emphasis on classroom interaction studies in the sociology of education has been of fundamental importance in illuminating the *processual* aspects of assessment in, for example, the formation of pupil careers, more recently, we have begun to see the emergence of studies which attempt to combine macro, and micro structural and processual perspectives. Such studies testify to the very powerful explanatory models which may be developed if sociologists are prepared to brave a course between the Scylla and Charybdis of the various perspectives.

The work of Sharp and Green already referred to provides a good example of such a broadening of perspective. The authors felt constrained to reject the interactionist model with which they started their study in favour of a Marxist interpretation of their data, since they found classroom perspectives alone could not explain their findings adequately.

Willis (1977) provides an even stronger case for the need to situate processual accounts of the development of pupil subcultures within the wider socio-economic structure of society. Like Hargreaves, Willis focuses on a 'delinquescent' group of low-achieving boys but relates their 'counter-culture' to the wider social class culture from which the boys come and which already exerts upon them a good measure of anticipatory socialization. The study identifies a correspondence between the boys' attitude to school and their existing and potential attitudes to work, both of which emphasize the importance of expressive relationships as found in the work group, humour and masculine chauvinism of the 'machismo' variety and in consequence involving a specific rejection of the individualistic, achievement-oriented value-system of the school. Thus, in contrast to Bourdieu's analysis in which the symbolic meanings of dominated social groups are submerged and obscured by the cultural arbitrary of the elite, Willis' boys retain their own cultural identity and perpetrate an identifiable if powerless opposition to the *status quo* of the school. Thus, for example, ignorance and under-achievement become a weapon against the dominant value set, to be positively displayed.

> The teacher's superiority is denied because the mode in which that superiority is expressed is delegitimated — there are other ways of valuing oneself. This valuation comes from those 'private' areas, now shared (i.e. in the counter-culture group) and made visible, which were held in check before. (Willis, 1976)

Perhaps the most significant argument in this analysis, though, is that it is the very rejection of school values and celebration of an alternative culture that perpetuates the system whereby 'working-class lads get working-class jobs'. Willis argues that it is the very strength of the lads identification with working-class culture and their own anticipated future jobs which brings about the reproduction of underprivilege much more systematically than any State-directed policy could and indeed the voluntary reproduction takes place in spite of, not because of, official State policy. Thus, it can be argued, the apparently *meritocratic* nature of an education system which in fact is so closely tied to the values and cultural norms of another class that it is all but meaningless to groups such as Willis' 'lads' socialized into a quite different class culture, serves a most important control and reproductive function. Not only does the apparent openness of the system legitimate it according to prevailing ideals of social justice as an appropriate and efficient mechanism of allocation in an industrialized and democratic society; it also ensures that the competition within the education system is significantly reduced by large numbers of pupils voluntarily opting out from the race. Thus, the pupils themselves 'do the work of bringing about the future others have mapped for them' (Willis, 1976). Keddie's (1971) argument is relevant here: that it is the willingness of 'high ability' pupils not to question what they are taught in schools but to be both able and willing to take over the teacher's definitions of what constitutes success, which contributes in great measure to their educational achievement. Like Willis she differentiates between the relevance of the school culture which perpetuates values of individual responsibility and competition for 'high ability' pupils destined for middle-class jobs, and its irrelevance for those whose working lives will be given meaning very largely by informal social relationships and who thus, in rejecting the values of the school, are inevitably identified as 'low-achievers'.

Summary

This chapter has sought to conceptualize the process of classroom assessment at several different levels. The inevitability of teachers assessing pupils and pupils assessing teachers informally has to be recognized. More significant is the fact that teachers' assessments have an exchange value but pupils' assessments, either of themselves or other people, do not. Teachers' assessments are given authority — are acted upon —

because they stand as guardians at the various entrances to the wider society, be they social or occupational. As such, assessment is of course a key mechanism of social control and vital to the efficient functioning of society as we know it. However, our analysis has also been at pains to reveal that pupils are constantly in receipt of evaluations according to existing (class) stereotypes from the moment they enter school and that the whole spectrum of assessment procedures, from the multiple-choice objective test at one end of the continuum to the covert non-cognitive evaluation at the other, embodies a particular set of cultural meanings. If such is the case, we have argued, pupils from particular cultural backgrounds will inevitably start at an advantage or disadvantage in all forms of assessment. We have seen too, how these initial handicaps are reinforced in classroom interaction and often result in pupils identifying *themselves* for the various ranks in the occupational hierarchy. In this sense, 'formative' assessment may make 'terminal' assessment unnecessary for discriminating amongst school-leavers. Rather the importance of terminal assessment, as we saw in chapter 3, is in maintaining the illusion of a fair fight in legitimating and making overt the process of selection.

We are thus brought to reject the dominant ideology of assessment as an instrument of social order and to substitute rather a perspective of assessment as an instrument of control, helping to reproduce the inequalities in society. Whether this must *inevitably* be so and whether assessment can have any more positive educational role are suitable questions for concluding our analysis and we shall turn to them in chapter 6.

6

Assessment
and social change

It has been one of the dominant themes of this book that educational assessment, perhaps more than any other aspect of education, has suffered the thraldom of 'methodological empiricism' in which questions of technique have effectively predominated over the more fundamental issue of its effects. We have sought to account for this state of affairs in the equally unquestioned domination of the liberal reformist ideology of education and the associated consensus view of society which likewise dominated sociology until recently. Hence the need for a rational and just means of 'role allocation' can be justified both pragmatically, in educational terms, as crucial to the establishment of a meritocracy and theoretically, in such functionalist sociological analysis, as necessary in a society characterized by a division of labour and social mobility. The acceptance of the assumptions contained in this ideology logically precludes the asking of certain questions.

Thus it is only the relatively recent developments of new *theoretical* perspectives in the sociology of education that have

118

enabled new questions about schooling to be formulated. Conflict, phenomenological and interpretive theories of society and social interaction, although highly significant in the development of new research techniques, have had an even more fundamental effect, as Gouldner (1971) asserts, in establishing new issues and new ways of interpreting data. As we have seen, these newer perspectives have tended to emphasize schooling as an agency of social control rather than of liberation and consequently have encouraged the formulation of new questions about the identification, transmission and evaluation of school knowledge.

By the same token it is possible to argue that the a-theoretical character of much of the educational research industry — so much deplored by C. Wright Mills in 1956, and still true today — has been highly instrumental in reinforcing the ideology currently underpinning education by unquestioningly accepting existing definitions of problems (Broadfoot, 1979b). The impact of the Rothschild Report (1971) in particular, which sought to establish educational research as a service industry in a market economy, can certainly be seen in this light and indeed, from a Marxist point of view, as an instance of alienation resulting from the intrusion of the social relationships of capitalist production into the production of knowledge itself.

However, much as we may criticize this model of educational research for operating on 'given' assumptions, it did have the major advantage of making a direct contribution to action for, as Karabel and Halsey (1977) point out, 'it leaves *ends* in the hands of policy-makers and concentrates the efforts of the social scientist on the means by which these ends may be obtained'. By contrast, the very shift towards more theoretically explicit research implies a greater commitment to action, and yet at the same time, makes that action less likely. If researchers move away from any claim to 'scientific objectivity' as such and recognize instead the inevitability of their work being 'contaminated' by their own interpretive paradigm and value-set (Hall, 1977), this very recognition that the apparently 'commonsense' assumptions informing their work are in fact 'political' will equally imply a commitment to a choice of one course of action in education over another. Becker (1967) puts it bluntly in

119

arguing that the issue cannot be 'how can we remain free from bias?' but must be 'whose side are we on?'

It is this very opening up of new perspectives in sociology and the consequent making explicit of theoretical positions that has produced apparently irreconcilable rifts between the various theoretical and methodological perspectives and is in danger of leading, according to Bernstein (1977), to a proliferation of ways — often mutually exclusive in the eyes of their propagators — of *approaching* problems at the expense of seeking for *solutions*. It is to the credit of the early sociology of education in Britain that for all its shortcomings, because it was united in a common cause, it was highly instrumental in achieving the reforms — such as the comprehensive school — its proponents sought. Now, when more than ever many sociologists are concerned to bring about change, they show less and less agreement about how such change may come about or what form it should take.

In this book my aim has been to raise the level of consciousness in thinking about assessment. It perhaps would have been easier to argue a coherent analysis of assessment from a particular perspective. Instead, though, I have adopted an essentially eclectic — one might even say dialectic — approach in that, as with any 'interdisciplinary' study, synthetic insights may emerge from the interaction and conflict between the various ways of looking at the topic. And indeed, it is perhaps in those areas of overlap between the various perspectives that the road to deeper insight lies. Certainly Apple and Wexler (1978) argue the potential of a rapprochement between the Durkheimian functionalist tradition and neo-Marxist insights such as that which characterizes the recent work of Bernstein who, in addition, has found it possible to apply the functionalist-oriented pattern-variables of Parsons such as 'universalistic' and 'particularistic' in a far from functionalist paradigm. The same interaction of perspectives is true of much of Bourdieu's work (Karabel and Halsey, 1977). Not only functionalists, but many neo-Marxists can similarly be criticized — as Althusser is by Erben and Gleeson (1975) — for assuming a positivistic interpretation of knowledge as being 'out there' and external to the learner who is perceived as passively manipulated by dominant mechanisms and social formations outside his control.

Erben and Gleeson (1975) provide another good example of the common ground between various conflict theorists and functionalists in their assumption of an essentially deterministic and static view of society. Thus they criticise Althusser's Marxist theory: 'it is a character of Althusser's *functionalist* method that the vocabulary of meanings belonging to the individual in a given situation is given no real attention and that therefore the potential situation for political activity is denied by scant attention and imprecise delineation.' It is the particular contribution of interpretive perspectives to re-establish the individual as a conscious actor once again. There is, however equally, the potential for complementary insights here between the Marxist emphasis on consciousness (McLellan, 1975) as a basis for collective action and the various interpretive perspectives' emphases on consciousness as the basis for individual action. The blurring of macro- and micro-perspectives — more difficult perhaps at the methodological level — is becoming increasingly necessary at the theoretical level.

Although we may seem to be a long way from assessment and social change — which is the subject of this chapter — the reason for this digression into more general issues can now I hope be made clear: I want, in this final part of the book, to look at assessment in ways that cut across conventional perspective boundaries, in drawing a more substantive distinction between assessment as socially-determined and assessment as socially-determining. Up to this point we have largely been concerned with exploring the development of assessment procedures as a response to the changing social demands made upon the education system. Assessment mechanisms have been seen as essentially determined by their functions in allocating individuals to the various levels of the social hierarchy and in legitimating that allocation in order to maintain social control. Innovation in assessment has thus tended to be seen as merely the reflection of a need for new modes of allocation or legitimation determined by social, political or economic changes.

If, however, we accept the legitimacy of interpretive perspectives too — of man as creator of his own reality (as in adopting an eclectic perspective we must) then it must be possible to see assessment in quite another way. If the actor himself had to define what constituted the appropriate realization of educational knowledge, then just as assessment in its current *modus operandi* reinforces the dominant culture, then equally it could come to legitimate and activate the alternative symbolic worlds — the alternative cultural meanings — of various individuals and groups. I am referring here to the power assessment procedures have to *legitimate* certain types of behaviour in the education system — certain forms of knowledge, certain skills, certain attributes — as of value educationally and, by the same token, to devalue other kinds of behaviour as worthless or even undesirable. If, as is happening in a few isolated experiments already, we allowed pupils and students *themselves* to define and assess achievement according to their own individual and group cultural values, we would be allowing them to legitimate in many cases a different and potentially conflictual system of school values, behavioural norms and curriculum content with all that that implies for the longer-term processes of social reproduction and social control. Although it is debatable whether such a change would result in a direct confrontation between the two economically-determined classes as in the Marxist view, or whether it would result in a more complex conflictual situation between a number of social groups, it is certain that in this sense assessment is a potentially radical instrument for social change. The point is perhaps best made by analysing further the political nature of assessment.

To innovate or not to innovate — a political question

As the bridge between school and society, assessment is arguably one of the most political aspects of education. (By political I mean here issues of social power and social control.) In chapter 4 we argued that formal assessment can be seen as a filter carefully designed, in form and content, to favour pupils who are best fitted to perpetuate society in its present form. We saw in chapter 5 how this process is only the visible tip of the huge iceberg of informal evaluation and channelling which goes on continually in the classroom and serves the same function (Jennings, 1974). It could conceivably be argued, taking a functionalist perspective, that the current international preoccupation with testing and accountability is a reflection, not of the failure of educational systems to 'deliver the goods', which is the reason given, but of the fact that they have been *too* successful in raising aspirations higher than opportunities; breaking down older systems of sponsored mobility (Turner, 1960) in favour of ever-expanding opportunity and 'contest' mobility; and teaching youngsters to question dominant values. As we saw in chapter 1, assessment comes increasingly into prominence as social control becomes more problematic and from both consensus and conflict perspectives it is apparent that new ways have to be found of maintaining the *status quo* and containing dissent whilst expanding opportunity. Thus, at all levels of assessment, from the most informal classroom interchange, through formal school evaluation to national and international issues of control and dominance in society, assessment is clearly political in that it helps to reinforce the constraints of a particular social reality.

Furthermore, it is unlikely, on the basis of this argument, that policy-makers, who are inevitably enmeshed in the need to preserve existing power structures, will seriously consider any reform in assessment procedures on the lines so frequently rehearsed by more maverick educationists, whose social value has a rather more flexible foundation. This has indeed proved to be the case. The voices of contemporary radicals such as John Holt or R.S. Mackenzie have fallen on the same deaf ears which have consistently refused to listen to the constant flow of both moral and technical criticisms of conventional assessment procedures throughout this century. This deafness is carefully disguised however, by the formation of large, influential committees representing an equally vested range of educational interests (Bourdieu and Passeron, 1976) which, once set up, either do not address the important issues at all or, although seen to be going through the motions, as it is in the nature of large committees only to reach a compromise at the point of the lowest common denominator, can safely be left to come to the right decision. This *apparent* discussion and consideration of the issues in a totally open way is, however, highly instrumental in rehearsing the case for the *status quo* and in obscuring the power relations involved. On the rare occasions when committees step out of line and seek to be genuinely innovatory, such as the

Report of the Advisory Council on Education in Scotland in 1947 or, in England, the Schools Council Report on *The Whole Curriculum, 13-16* in 1975, a choice of strategies is open to political interests seeking to maintain the *status quo*, ranging from accepting the recommendations but delaying their implementation indefinitely because of apparent practical problems, to ignoring or quietly overruling them. Typically, though, public committees on assessment, even if, like the Beloe Committee in 1960, they have reservations, limit themselves to discussions within the parameters laid down by the politicians. The two most recent major reports on public assessment in Britain: the Dunning Committee in Scotland (1977) and the Waddell Committee in England (1978), are both good examples. In the Dunning Report we find:

> The point has been made that all pupils should be included in assessments with the aim of improving individual performance or providing curricular and vocational guidance. An assessment system limited to these teaching and guidance aims could be assembled relatively quickly and economically, with the concentration of effort on national support for the teacher in classroom assessment.... In such a system information on individual performance would be confined to internal use. However, we recognize that public certification is regarded as an important purpose of assessment, since it provides pupils with a target and nationally validated record of individual achievements and the qualification for entry to either tertiary education or employment....

And in the Waddell Report:

> We were aware of general questions which are often debated concerning the need for, and place of, examinations in society and the imperfections which are inherent in the nature of any system of examining. As a Committee we were not constituted, nor had we time, to re-examine and come to view on all these broad issues as they merit, although we kept them in mind as a background to our work. In the circumstances we did, however, accept that public examination would remain an essential feature of our educational system for the foreseeable future.

So, as policy-makers give every evidence of being firmly wedded to reformism, we cannot look to them for any conception of assessment as a determinant of fundamental educational and eventually social change. But is there a case for change anyway?

Many academics have given the lead in showing that, given commitment to the very widely held view that education should be a means of personal development and intellectual growth, change is not only desirable but essential. Rée (1977) deplores what 'this obsession with examinations has already done to our whole education system, to the motivation of students who see their degree course as little more than a race for a piece of paper, to the morale of teachers, who have better things to do than train intellectual hurdlers, and to the whole concept of scholarship and education as a worthwhile end in itself'. To these criticisms, we might add those of the School of Barbiana (1970):

> You [the teacher] work 210 days a year, of which thirty are lost in giving exams and over thirty more on tests. That leaves only 150 days of school in a year. Half of these schooldays are lost in oral examinations which means that there are seventy-five days of teaching against 135 of passing judgement....

Add to this the cost of formal assessment. In 1976 the cost of O-level and CSE examinations alone amounted to £13.5 million pounds, an average of £2.40 per subject entry. Indeed public exams may be regarded as one of the few remaining growth industries! That change is desirable is hard to refute. That it is possible is a much more problematic question and raises again the dilemma integral to industrial mass society identified in chapter 1. The answer must lie in the first instance in a sociological understanding of the potential for change in society.

Reformist versus radical change

In order to begin to answer this question, however, it is important to define what we mean by change, and so I shall draw a distinction between 'soft' change and 'hard' change — to use popular jargon. By this I mean on the one hand relatively superficial changes in practice which effect the process of schooling and, on the other, fundamental changes in assessment practice which are born out of a very different conception of schooling and the hierarchical power relations and knowledge currently embedded in it.

Most of the arguments for assessment reform are of the 'soft' variety. De-schoolers, progressives and liberals combine in denouncing the constraints of examinations, the alienative effects of failure, the devaluing of a conception of education for its own sake. Through reforms in assessment, they believe, aspiration, motivation, confidence and involvement can be improved. The reforms envisaged include the abandoning of formal testing altogether — as in many primary schools; the substitution of criterion-referenced for norm-referenced testing, so that children do not compete against each other; the growing emphasis on diagnostic assessment; and the broadening of the content of assessment so that all types of achievement — personal, social and academic — are valued and success in some aspect of school life is possible for every child (SCRE, 1977).

All these changes should help to make the learning process less threatening, more personalized and hence more productive for pupils and as such are to be welcomed. Bloom (1974), for example, has demonstrated empirically that students actually become better able to learn as a result of the experience of mastery. Adams and Burgess (1979) provide many examples of innovations in assessment practices which testify to the ground swell towards 'soft' changes currently taking place in schools.

It is vital to point out, however, that as we saw in chapter 3, such changes can in no sense be seen as socially or politically radical. Rather they provide firstly, as Bernstein (1975) argues, new ways of differentiating between individuals, more appropriate to the changing class structure of society, and secondly, a way of 'sugaring the pill' of schooling and particularly of selection. They are thus highly instrumental in maintaining social control. At one level we may welcome such changes in that they certainly allow assessment to reinforce the whole range of teaching objectives (Raven, 1977). Similarly, we may welcome another significant change identified in chapter 3, and that is the postponement of selection. Both qualification inflation and the

126

liberal ideology's elevation of formal education as a common good have led to more and more students throughout the world staying on at school after the end of compulsory schooling — which in itself is tending to become longer and longer. It is conceivable that in developed countries at least and as some countries have already done, formal assessment at the end of compulsory schooling and more importantly, selection, may be abandoned as unnecessary. Indeed there are signs that it may not be too long before all formal selection will be postponed to the post-secondary stage entirely, with a consequent lengthening of higher education courses to allow for a lower standard of entrant and 'in' rather than 'pre' course selection. University failure rates in the United States and France for example are existing examples of such practice and the call by the Vice-Chancellor of Liverpool University at the 1978 Headmasters' Conference (Whelan, 1978) for all honours degree courses to become four years rather than the (in England) more normal three years, in order to 'maintain' standards, may be evidence of a similar recognition in England of qualification inflation and the trend to postponing selection.

Certainly the liberation of the compulsory schooling stage at least from formal assessment would enable a much sharper distinction to be drawn between general mass education — the old elementary education in many ways or the 'basic' school in Scandinavia — and the more specialized, voluntary courses embarked upon after this stage. Certainly this latter stage, even if provided in a common 'tertiary' or 'secondary' college — and some boroughs in England are already experimenting with this idea — would be no freer of the class biases in aspiration and achievement currently operating in schools. It would, though, go some way to freeing the 'comprehensive' part of schooling from the exigencies of norm-referenced accreditation. Although to some extent such a scheme would constitute an extended primary school and the liberation since the Plowden Report that that has come to imply, it would be yet more significant in that it would mean a good number of children going through education from start to finish with no experience of selection and formal assessment and rather more likely to have had an experience of freedom and personal responsibility for learning which will be positive enough to encourage them to pursue education further.

Inevitably, these suggestions sound rather glib. So much must remain hypothetical until research into such alternatives can be undertaken since, as we have seen, most of the research so far available concentrates on a narrow vision of doing better what we are currently doing. More than anything, empirical research is needed to widen the debate about assessment. If, at the very least, further evidence were available on the power structures involved in policy-making, the ideologies governing bodies involved in public assessment such as the Schools Council and the Examination Boards and in the assessment practices of other countries, this would make a major contribution. At the micro-level too, more research is needed into the scope and effects of different assessment practices in individual classrooms. Such studies could not only illuminate assessment as a manifestation of classroom interaction but could be instrumental in the search for new ways of influencing that interaction in order to overcome some of the existing barriers to the achievement of educational objectives.

It would be wrong, however, to expect very spectacular results from 'soft' changes in assessment practice. Certainly the United States, whose school system is one of the least dominated by formal assessment and selection, is not distinguished for its lack of illiterates, truants, drop-outs and differential social and ethnic group achievement. Many 'Black Paperites' would argue, too, that we invite 'falling standards' by such tactics. These are of course all highly complex issues involving many other aspects of education than assessment alone. The crux of the 'soft' changes argument is simply that there do seem to be grounds for anticipating the development of assessment procedures, both formal and informal, which will be more closely geared to a defined educational philosophy and which may well make the experience of 'basic' schooling a more rewarding one than at present for many pupils. At the same time, however, it is important to stress that such innovations are most likely to come about *simply because* they reinforce the existing social hierarchies and power structure.

The alternative 'hard' changes in assessment are those which would allow assessment procedures to have a potential role in social change. To explain this we need to invoke Freire's (1972) use of the Marxian concept of praxis as the basis for genuine education. To risk over-simplifying a complex argument, Freire regards education as a part of the individual's interaction with his environment as a result of which he builds up his own unique understanding of the world. A teacher cannot therefore teach the child a pre-existing body of knowledge but can only join with him in his voyage of discovery. As a result of such education, Freire argues, the individual becomes intimately in touch with his own reality, his own set of meanings— a process which he terms 'conscientization' and regards as a political process because it allows the development amongst individuals of an awareness of their own conditions and culture vis-à-vis that dominant in society. In Freire's vision of an alternative education, the dominant culture cannot be imposed through the curriculum, pedagogy and evaluation systems of the school because these are not externally imposed but are created by the learners as individuals or groups. 'It is not a situation where one knows and others do not; it is rather the search, by all, at the same time to discover something by the act of knowing which cannot exhaust all the possibilities in the relation between object and subject' (Freire, 1971). Hence a political conflict — a conflict over the right to maintain opposing interpretations of reality — is inevitably indicated.

Freire's theories, born in the very different social situation of the slums of Brazil, will probably be seen by most Western educators as both unfeasible and undesirable. However they do illuminate a possible way in which assessment could be instrumental in bringing about social change. In practice this would mean giving the responsibility for the content and method of study and its evaluation to the learner himself. By so doing, we would establish praxis in learning, allowing the pupil to define issues and learning tasks through the interpretation mediated by his own culture; to retain the essential creativity of all kinds of labour in using a range of skills at his own discretion and in not alienating the learner from the products of his labour by putting an external (commodity) value on it in the form of marks and grades rooted in dominant cultural standards. By allowing the learner himself to create rather than receive knowledge he will

129

develop his own critical consciousness and a valuation system based on a dynamic interrelationship between his own experience and the wider reality of history.

There are signs that experiments along these lines in both curriculum and assessment are already taking place. Stephenson (1979) writes of successful experiments in individual course design and self-initiated evaluation categories for the Dip HE at the North East London Polytechnic School of Independent Study. Some degree courses, such as the Southampton University B.Ed, involve substantial individually- or group-determined curriculum and evaluation components. Some schools, such as Countesthorpe College and the Sutton Centre, have made a start with individualized curricula even if external evaluation is still a constraint. Innovations in school certification in the form of the Record of Personal Achievement and now the Record of Personal Experience (Stansbury, 1979), which document only what the pupil feels is significant to him and worthy of recording, is another significant step in the same direction. How far such developments are likely to be allowed to go before they begin to be a threat is an open question. That they are a threat to the *status quo* is certain. To the extent that a pupil, rather than opting out of an alien educational system in the way Willis (1977) describes, identifies instead his own learning objectives and performs his own assessment in accordance with a different set of cultural values to those currently established in the school, he represents a threat to all the common-sense categories defining what education is in industrial society and hence indirectly, to the dominant social order. This is essentially a political threat. Almost by definition, allowing individuals and groups to emphasize a different set of cultural meanings in their learning (groups will share cultural meanings to the extent that they share social experience) to those of the dominant group, will be likely, in time, to remove one of the major mechanisms of reproducing the social order and instead encourage conflicting definitions of what should constitute that order. The need for such conflict as a precursor to the overthrow of capitalism is, of course, central to Marxist theory and hence will be welcomed by all who adopt this theory of society in one or other of its forms, even if it is not always entirely clear how such

130

conflict is to come about. Taking a broader view of social consciousness as the product of differential cultural experiences influenced by geographic, ethnic, sexual, familial and religious as well as economic factors, then prognostications about the results of 'conscientized' education are much harder to predict. If each social group is enabled to pursue praxical learning — learning involving the creative exploration of its own reality and evaluation according to a critical consciousness embedded in its own experience of, and influence on, that reality — it is possible to envisage a major disintegration — indeed anarchy — in the political order. And in fact, there is no reason to suppose that ascendant groups would not seek to impose their own value- and status-systems on others in the society.

A more likely situation in practice, however, is that the influence of the international technocratic culture is sufficient to induce an *international uniformity* of educational values. Since almost without exception both developed and developing nations want to compete in the international market economy geared to highly technicalized production and capitalist economic relations, this has led all over the world to striking similarities in educational practice, the rationale reflecting technocratic imperatives rather than the culture of any one social group (Broadfoot, 1978b). Although these highly complex issues go well beyond the scope of assessment procedures alone and are concerned with the determined and determining nature of the education system as a whole in relation to society, assessment procedures are highly significant in their common emphasis throughout the world on intellectual and academic specialization, 'meritocratic' selection and the importance of qualifications.

It seems likely that this 'world educational culture' (with few exceptions), born of capitalism and the industrial and technological revolutions, will perpetrate the liberal reformist ideology on a world scale — with all that that implies. Innovations in assessment procedures in communist countries, including, in particular, a much greater emphasis on testing for cognitive skills and on academic selection for higher education, show clearly how their educational ideology is increasingly being influenced by the 'technological imperative'. Thus although it

131

has been possible to conceptualize assessment as an instrument of social change, it is hard to ignore the overwhelming odds against assessment being used in this way. Certainly any significant innovation is unlikely to be instituted at a macro, structural level and thus will have to start at the level of innovation by the individual teacher in the classroom. It is just conceivable that the combined effect of a number of such piecemeal initiatives would be a change in the prevailing definitions of 'legitimate practice', leading through a gradual change in consciousness to the development of a new ideology of learning and evaluation. Perhaps the best we can hope for in the foreseeable future however is a greater emphasis on 'soft' changes in assessment. For it is indisputable that the more the liberal reformist ideology predominates, the more the goal of the meritocracy is enshrined, the more emphasis will be placed on assessment procedures to provide foolproof ways of identifying merit. Bearing in mind too the evidence presented in this book and elsewhere of the strong influence exerted by assessment procedures on the process of education, there is a good case to be made for concentrating efforts to change the educational system on assessment procedures. Running through all the chapters of this book has been the contradiction between education as a creator of opportunity and education as the mediation of control and the role of assessment as vital in both respects. If the education system has indeed been one of the major forces of social reproduction in modern industrial society as well as a major force for social liberation, then educational assessment must be seen as one of the major means of justifying the continual distinctions between rich and poor, powerful and weak. For, as Marx perhaps could not foresee, writing in a less secular age, *assessment*, far more than religion, has become 'the opiate of the people' (Marx, 1957).

References and
name index

Adams, E. and Burgess, T. (eds) (1979) *Outcomes of Education*. London: Macmillan *126*

Advisory Council on Education in Scotland (1947) *Secondary Education*. Edinburgh: HMSO *124*

Apple, M.W. and Wexler, P. (1978) Cultural capital and educational transmissions: an essay on Basil Bernstein, *Class Codes and Control*, Vol III — *towards a theory of educational transmission. Educational Theory 28*, no 1: 34-44 *114, 120*

Armytage, W.H.G. (1964) *Four Hundred Years of English Education*. Cambridge University Press

Assessment of Performance Unit (1977) *Assessment, Why, What and How?* London: HMSO *75*

Bacharach, P. and Baratz, M.S. (1962) The two faces of power. *American Political Science Review 56*, December *27, 54*

Barbiana School (1970) *Letter to a Teacher*. Harmondsworth: Penguin *73, 125*

Barnard, H.C. (1961) *A History of English Education from 1760*.

University of Liverpool Press   *30*

Becher, T. and Maclure, S. (1978) *The Politics of Curriculum Change*. London: Hutchinson   *79, 97*

Becker, H. (1967) Whose side are we on? *Social Problems 14*: 239-47   *119*

Becker, H. (1976) The career of the Chicago public school teacher. In M. Hammersley and P. Woods (eds) *The Process of Schooling*. London: Routledge & Kegan Paul   *112*

Beeby, C.E. (1966) *The Quality of Education in Developing Countries*. Oxford University Press   *57*

Bell, R. and Grant, N. (1974) *A Mythology of British Education*. London: Panther   *29*

Bellaby, P. (1977) *The Sociology of Comprehensive Schooling*. London: Methuen   *92*

Benn, C. (1978) *Times Educational Supplement*, 10.2.1978   *60*

Benn, C. and Simon, B. (1970) *Half-Way There: Report of the British Comprehensive School Reform*. Harmondsworth: Penguin   *60*

Bernstein, B. (1970) Education cannot compensate for society. *New Society* 26.2.1970: 344-7   *111*

Bernstein, B. (1971) *Class Codes and Control*, Vol. 1. London: Routledge & Kegan Paul   *18, 105*

Bernstein, B. (1975) Class and pedagogies: visible and invisible. *Educational Studies 1* no 1, March   *126*

Bernstein, B. (1977) *Class Codes and Control*, Vol. III. London: Routledge & Kegan Paul   *71, 101, 120*

Binyon, M. (1976) Equality or quality. *Times Educational Supplement*, 19.3.76   *69, 73*

Block, J.H. (1971) Criterion-reference measurements: potential. *School Review 79*: 289-98   *54*

Bloom, B.S. (1971) *Individual Differences in School Achievement: A Vanishing Point?* Bloomington, Indiana: Phi Delta Kappa   *54*

Bloom, B. (1974) Time and learning. *American Psychologist*, September: 682-8   *126*

Board of Education (1911) *Report of the Consultative Committee on Examinations in Secondary School*. London: HMSO   *33, 34, 38*

Bonavia, D. (1978) Clock turned back to improve standards.

Times Educational Supplement, 19.5.78 *26, 74*

Bourdieu, P. (1971) Systems of education and systems of thought. In M.F.D. Young (ed.) *Knowledge and Control*. London: Collier Macmillan *111*

Bourdieu, P. (1974) The school as a conservative force: scholastic and cultural inequalities. In J. Eggleston (ed.) *Contemporary Research in the Sociology of Education*. London: Methuen *16, 98*

Bourdieu, P. and Passeron, J.C. (1976) *Reproduction in Education, Society and Culture*. London: Sage *20, 34, 40, 64, 98, 112, 123*

Bowles, S. and Gintis, H. (1976) *Schooling in Capitalist America*. London: Routledge & Kegan Paul *39, 48, 69, 94, 95*

Bowles, S. and Gintis, H. (1977) IQ in the U.S. class structure. In D. Gleeson (ed.) *Identity and Structure*. Driffield: Nafferton Books *101*

Broadfoot, P. (1978a) The near monopoly of one kind of mind. *Times Educational Supplement* (Scotland), 6.1.78 *52, 88*

Broadfoot, P. (1978b) *The Politics of Radical Education*. Paper given to W. Midlands Open University Sociology Society, June *99, 131*

Broadfoot, P. (1979a) Communication in the classroom: a study of the role of assessment in motivation. *Educational Review* *31*, no 1, Feb: pp. 3-11 *71*

Broadfoot, P. (1979b) Educational research through the looking glass. *Scottish Educational Review*. Autumn *119*

Broadfoot, P. (1979c) The Scottish pupil profile system. In E. Adams and T. Burgess (eds) *Outcomes of Education*. London: Macmillan *33*

Brown, Alan (1975) Recruitment standards for school leavers. *Trends in Education*, Summer *69*

Brown, S. and McIntyre, D. (1977) *Differences among pupils in science classes: the contrast between teachers' perceptions and pupils' performance*. Paper presented to Scottish Educational Research Association, St Andrews *24, 108, 111*

Bruce, G. (1969) *Secondary School Examinations — Facts and Commentary*. London: Pergamon Press

Burstall, C. and Kay, B. (1978) *Assessment — The American Experience*. London: HMSO *77, 78*

135

Burt, Sir Cyril (1912) The inheritance of mental characteristics. *Eugenics Review 4(2)*: 168-200 *44*

Burt, Sir Cyril, Jones, E. *et al*. (eds) (1933) *How the Mind Works*. London: Allen & Unwin *44*

Central Advisory Council for Education (England) (1959) *15 to 18* (The Crowther Report). London: HMSO *33*

Central Advisory Council for Education (1967) *Children and Their Primary Schools* (The Plowden Report). London: HMSO *47*

Central Advisory Council for Education (England) (1968) *Half Our Future* (The Newsom Report). London: HMSO

Central Council for Education (1977) *Interim Outline of the U90 Plan*. Copenhagen *68*

Chomsky, N. (1977) IQ tests: building blocks for the new class system. In B. Cosin *et al*. (eds) *School and Society*. London: Routledge & Kegan Paul *49*

Cicourel, A.V. (1974) Assessment of performance— some basic theoretical issues. In A.V. Cicourel, K.H. and S.H.M. Jennings, K.C.W. Leiter, R. Mackay, H. Mehan and D.R. Roth *Language Use and School Performance*. New York: Academic Press *104*

Clark, B. (1962) *Educating the Expert Society*. San Francisco: Chandler Publishing Co.

Coleman, J. *et al*. (1966) *Equality of Educational Opportunity*. Washington DC: US Government Printing Office *26*

Coleman, J. (1968) The concept of equality of educational opportunity. *Harvard Educational Review* (special issue) Winter, 38(1): 7-22 *26*

Cookson, C. (1978) Testing, testing, testing. *Times Educational Supplement*, 10.2.78 *73*

Consultative Committee to the Board of Education (1926) *The Education of the Adolescent* (The Hadow Report). London: HMSO *45, 46*

Consultative Committee on Education (1938) *Secondary Education* (The Spens Report). London: HMSO *38, 45, 88*

Council of Europe (1977) *Sweden: Proposals for the Modification of School Assessment Procedures*. Newsletter, Feb. 1977 *62*

Council of Europe (1978) *Norway: Assessment at School*. Newsletter, Jan. 1978 *62*

Cox, C.B. and Dyson, A.E. (1969a) (eds) *Fight for Education* (Black Paper). London: The Critical Quarterly Society *79*

Cox, C.B. and Dyson, A.E. (1969b) (eds) *The Crisis in Education* (Black Paper). London: The Critical Quarterly Society *79*

Cox, C.B. and Dyson, A.E. (1970) (eds) *Goodbye Mr Short* (Black Paper). London: The Critical Quarterly Society *79*

Cox, C.B. and Dyson, A.E. (1975) *The Fight for Education* (Black Paper 4) London: Dent *79*

Cox, C.B. and Dyson, A.E. (1977) *Black Paper 5*. London: Temple Smith *79*

Dale, R. (1977) Implications of the rediscovery of the hidden curriculum for the sociology of teaching. In D. Gleeson (ed.) *Identity and Structure*. Driffield: Nafferton Books *96*

Davidson, H.H. and Lang, G. (1960) Children's perceptions of their teachers' feelings towards them related to self-perception, school achievement and behaviour. *Journal of Experimental Education 29*, no 2: 107-18 *113*

Dennison, W.F. (1978) Research Report: The Assessment of Performance Unit — Where is it leading? *Durham and Newcastle Research Review VIII*, no 40 *75*

DES (1977) *Education in Schools* (Green Paper) (Cmnd 6869). London: HMSO *77*

DES (1978) *School Examinations: Report of the steering committee established to consider proposals for replacing the G.C.E. O-level and C.S.E. examinations by a common system of examining* (The Waddell Report). London: HMSO *124*

Dore, R. (1976) *The Diploma Disease*. London: Unwin Education Books *31, 34, 54, 60, 80*

Douglas, J.W.B. (1964) *The Home and the School*. London: MacGibbon & Kee *47, 110*

Duckenfield, M. (1977) Are good marks worth getting? *Times Educational Supplement 68*

Dundas-Grant, V. (1975) Attainment at 16+: the French perspective. *Comparative Education II*, no 1, March: 13-22

Dungworth, D. (1977) Lottery may choose students. *Times Educational Supplement*, 4.3.77 *62*

Durkheim, E. (1969) *L'évolution pédagogique en France*. Presses Universitaires de France *96*

Eggleston, J. (1979) Comparing and contrasting comprehensive and selection systems of education. In M.D. Carelli and J.G. Morris (eds) *Equality of Opportunity Reconsidered: Values in Education for Tomorrow*. Lisse: Swets & Zeitlinger   *64*

Erben, M. and Gleeson, D. (1975) Reproduction and social structure: Comments on Louis Althusser's Sociology of Education. *Educational Studies 1* no 2: 121-7   *120, 121*

Erickson, S.A. (1970) *Language and Being: An Analytic Phenomenology*. New Haven and London: Yale University Press   *104*

Esland, G. (1977) *Diagnosis and Testing*. Unit 21 Course E202. Milton Keynes: The Open University   *48*

Fairhall, J. (1978) Testing time — an investigation of school examinations. *The Guardian*, 8-10.2.78   *35*

Finn, D., Grant, N. and Johnson, R. (1977) Social democracy, education and the crisis. *Cultural Studies 10: On ideology 92*

Fleming, E.S. and Anttonen, R.G. (1971) Teacher expectancy or my fair lady. *AERA Journal 8*   *106*

Forsyth, J.P. and Dockrell, W.B. (1979) *Curriculum & Assessment for 14 to 16 year olds in Scottish Secondary Schools: A Case Study of Reaction to the Mum & Dunning Reports*. Edinburgh: SCRE   *57*

Freire, P. (1971) A few notions about the word 'conscientization'. *Hard Cheese 1:* 23-8   *99, 129*

Freire, P. (1972) *Education as Cultural Action*. Harmondsworth: Penguin   *99, 129*

Gardner, J. (1978) Great leap back to basics. *Times Educational Supplement*, 21.4.78   *88*

Giles, K. and Woolfe, R. (1977) *Deprivation, Disadvantage and Compensation*. Unit 25-6 Course E202. Milton Keynes: The Open University   *49*

Gloriozov, P.A. (1974) Preparing and administering school-leaving examinations. *Soviet Education 16:* 165-72   *61*

Good, T.L. and Brophy, J.E. (1970) Teacher-child dyadic interactions: a new method of classroom observation. *Journal of School Psychology 8*, no 2: 131-8   *109*

Goody, J. and Watt, I. (1962) The consequences of literacy.

Comparative Studies in History and Society 5, no 3   98
Gouldner, A.W. (1971) *The Coming Crisis of Western Sociology*. London: Heinemann   *119*
Greany, V. and Kellaghan, T. (1972) Cognitive and personality factors associated with the class placement of pupils. *Irish Journal of Education 6*, Winter   *107*
Gretton, J. and Jackson, M. (1976) *William Tyndale: Collapse of a School — or a System?* London: Allen & Unwin   *20*

Hall, S. (1977) *Review of the course*. E202 Unit 32. Milton Keynes: The Open University   *92, 119*
Halsey, A.H. and Gardner, L. (1953) Selection for secondary education. *British Journal of Sociology*, March   *47*
Halsey, A.H. (1972) *Educational Priority*, Vol 1 *EPA Problems and Policies*. London: HMSO   *95*
Halsey, A.H. (1978) Change in British society: The Reith Lectures. *The Listener*, January/February   *48, 94*
Hargreaves, D.H. (1967) *Social Relations in a Secondary School*. London: Routledge & Kegan Paul   *41, 114*
Hargreaves, D. (1976) Reactions to labelling. In M. Hammersley and P. Woods (eds) *The Process of Schooling*. London: Routledge & Kegan Paul   *113*
Hartog, Sir Philip and Rhodes, E.C. (1935) *An Examination of Examinations*. London: Macmillan   *22, 38, 88*
Henderson, P. (1976) Class structure and the concept of intelligence. In R. Dale *et al.* (eds) *Schooling and Capitalism*. London: Routledge & Kegan Paul   *49, 50*
HM Inspectorate (1978) *Primary Education in England*. London: HMSO   *78*
Hextall, I. (1976) Marking work. In G. Whitty and M. Young (eds) *Explorations in the Politics of School Knowledge*. Driffield: Nafferton Books   *93, 96*
Hextall, I. and Sarup, M. (1977) School knowledge, evaluation and alienation. In M. Young and G. Whitty (eds) *Society, State and Schooling*. Ringmer: The Falmer Press   *93*
Hill, B. (1976) Staff threaten boycotts to end entry exams. *Times Higher Education Supplement*   *67*
Holly, D. (1976) A starting point for liberation. In J. MacBeath (ed.) *A Question of Schooling*. London: Hodder & Stoughton   *81*

Holt, J. (1969) Schools are bad places for kids. *Saturday Evening Post*, Feb. 1969. Reprinted in *The Underachieving School*. Harmondsworth: Pelican (1970) *96*

Holmes, E. (1911) *What is and what might be* *33*

Hoste, R. and Bloomfield, B. (1975) *Continuous Assessment in the CSE: Opinion and Practice*. Schools Council Examinations Bulletin 31. London: Evans/Methuen Educational *42, 108*

Illich, I. (1971) *Deschooling Society*. London: Calder & Boyars *99*

Ingenkamp, K. (1977) *Educational Assessment*. Windsor: NFER for Council of Europe *74, 88*

Jackson, B. (1964) *Streaming: An Education System in Miniature*. London: Routledge & Kegan Paul *110*

Jackson, P.W. (1968) *Life in Classrooms*. Holt, Rinehart & Winston *107, 113*

Jencks, C. (1972) *Inequality: A Reassessment of the Effect of Family and Schooling in America*. New York: Basic Books *64*

Jennings, K. and S. (1974) Tests and experiments with children. In Cicourel *et al. Language Use and School Performance*. New York: Academic Press *122*

Johnson, R. (1976) Notes on the schooling of the English working class 1780-1850. In Dale *et al*. (eds) *Schooling and Capitalism*. London: Routledge & Kegan Paul *30, 51*

Journal Officiel (1977), décret No 77.918 and arrêté 2.8.77. *Le BEPC en 1978*. Paris *62*

Kamin, L.J. (1974) *The Science and Politics of IQ*. New York: Wiley *44, 50, 92*

Karabel, J. and Halsey, A.H. (1977) (eds) *Power and Ideology in Education*. New York: Oxford University Press *87, 90, 119, 120*

Karier, C.J. *et al*. (eds) (1973) *Roots of Crisis*. Chicago: Rand McNally *49*

Katz, M.B. (1965) From Bryce to Newsom: assumptions of British educational reports, 1895-1963. *International Review of Education*, Vol. 11: 287-302 *25*

Keddie, N. (1971) Classroom knowledge. In M.F.D. Young

(ed.) *Knowledge and Control*. London: Collier Macmillan *35, 110, 116*

Kelly, A. (1976) *The Comparability of Examining Standards in the Scottish Certificate of Education Ordinary and Higher Grade Examinations*. Edinburgh: SCEEB *40*

Kelly, P.J. (1971) Re-appraisal of examinations. *Journal of Curriculum Studies 3*, no 2 *88*

King, E. (1967) *Other Schools and Ours*. London: Holt, Rinehart & Winston *68*

Kogan, M. (1978) *The Politics of Educational Change*. London: Fontana *97*

Kuhn, T. (1970) *The Structure of Scientific Revolutions*. University of Chicago Press *89*

Lambart, A. (1976) The sisterhood. In M. Hammersley and P. Woods (eds) *The Process of Schooling*. London: Routledge & Kegan Paul *114*

Lauwerys, J.A. and Scanlon, D.G. (eds) (1969) *Examinations. The World Year Book of Education 1969*. London: Evans *88*

Lawson, J. and Silver, H. (1973) *A Social History of Education in England*. London: Methuen *31, 36*

Lister, I. (1974) (ed.) *Deschooling*. Cambridge University Press *88*

Lowndes, G.A.N. (1969) *The Silent Social Revolution*. Oxford University Press *38*

McHugh, P. *et al*. (1974) *On the Beginning of Social Enquiry*. London: Routledge & Kegan Paul *93*

McIntosh, H.G. (1974) (ed.) *Techniques and Problems of Assessment*. London: Edward Arnold *100*

Mackay, R. (1974) Standardized tests: objective/objectified measures of competence. In Cicourel *et al*., *op. cit*. *105*

McLellan, D. (1975) *Marx*. London: Fontana *121*

Maclure, J. Stuart (1965) *Educational Documents in England and Wales 1816–1967*. London: Methuen *31, 48*

Maguire, J. (1976) *An Outline of Assessment Methods in Secondary Education in Selected Countries*. Edinburgh: Scottish Council for Research in Education *66, 74*

Marjoram, T. (1977) Patience rewarded — a report on the

141

progress of the Assessment of Performance Unit. *Times Educational Supplement*, 14.10.77 *19, 67, 75*

Marx, K. (1957) Contribution to critique of Hegel's philosophy of right. In Marx and Engels (eds) *On religion*. London: Progress Publishers *132*

Midwinter, E. (1970) *Nineteenth-Century Education*. Seminar Studies in History. London: Longman *51*

Ministry of Education (1945) *The Nation's Schools*. London: HMSO *37*

Ministry of Education (1977) *Education in Schools: A Consultative Document*. London: HMSO *77*

Montgomery, R.J. (1965) *Examinations: An Account of their Evolution as Administrative Devices in England*. Harlow: Longman *31*

Morrison, A. (1974) Formal and informal assessment in the classroom. *Education in the North*: 63-7 *108, 112*

Musgrave, P.W. (1968) *Society and Education in England since 1800*. London: Methuen *35, 42*

Nash, R. (1974) Pupils' expectations for their teachers. *Research in Education* *110*

Nash, R. (1976) *Teacher Expectation and Pupil Learning*. London: Routledge & Kegan Paul *110*

Neave, G. (1979) Statements at 16: A European Perspective. In E. Adams and T. Burgess (eds) *Outcomes of Education*. London: Macmillan *65, 66, 68, 74, 80*

Nuttall, D.L., Backhouse, J.K. and Wilmott, A.S. (1974) *Comparability of Standards Between Subjects*. Schools Council Examination Bulletin 29. London: Evans/Methuen Educational *40*

OECD (1969) *Development of Secondary Education: Trends and Implications*. Paris: OECD *64*

Parsons, T. (1959) The school class as a social system: some of its functions in American society. *Harvard Educational Review 29* (Fall): 297-318 *107*

Partridge, J. (1968) *Life in a Secondary Modern School*. Harmondsworth: Pelican *41, 46*

Pidgeon, D. and Yates, A. (1968) *An Introduction to Educational Measurement*. London: Routledge & Kegan Paul 88

Popham, W.J. and Husek, T.R. (1969) Implications of criterion-referenced measurement. *Journal of Educational Measurement 6*, no 1: 1-9 54

Powell, J.L. (1973) *Selection for University in Scotland*. Edinburgh: ULP for SCRE 22

Price, R. (1976) Community and school, and education in the People's Republic of China. *Comparative Education 12*, no 2, June 69

Price, R. (1977) *Marx and Education in Russia and China*. London: Croom Helm 69

Raven, J. (1977) *Education, Values and Society*. London: H.K. Lewis *80, 97, 126*

Rée, H. (1977) Black marks for Boyson's own paper. *Sunday Observer*, February *125*

Rist, R.C. (1970) Student social class and teacher expectations: the self-fulfilling prophecy in ghetto education. *Harvard Educational Review 40*, no 3: 411-511 *110*

Roach, J. (1971) *Public exams in England 1850-1906*. CUP *32, 36, 52*

Robinson, P. (1977) Poverty and education: a pragmatic circle. In D. Gleeson (ed.) *Identity and Structure* Driffield: Nafferton Books *93*

Rogers, V. (1978) When relevance is a dirty word. *Times Educational Supplement*, 28.4.78 *88*

Rosenthal, R. and Jacobsen, L. (1968) *Pygmalion in the Classroom*. New York: Holt, Rinehart & Winston *111*

Roth, D.R. (1974) Intelligence testing as a social activity. In A.V. Cicourel, K.H. and S.H.M. Jennings, S.C.W. Leiter, R. Mackay and H. Mehan, D.R. Roth *Language Use and School Performance*. New York: Academic Press *105*

Rothschild, N.H.V.R., 3rd Baron (1971) *The Organization and Management of Government Research and Development — A Framework*. Presented to Parliament *119*

Rowan, P. (1976) Slow, slow, quick, quick, slow. *Times Educational Supplement*, 1.9.76 *61*

Rowntree, D. (1977) *Assessing students: How Shall We Know*

143

Them. London: Harper & Row   *36, 100*

Rubinstein, D. and Simon, B. (1969) *The Evolution of the Comprehensive School 1926-1966*. London: Routledge & Kegan Paul   *39, 45, 60*

Ryrie, A.C. and Weir, A.D. (1978) *Getting a Trade — A Study of Apprentices, Experience of Apprenticeship*. London: Hodder & Stoughton, for Scottish Council for Research in Education   *31*

Schools Council (1975) *The Whole Curriculum, 13-16*. Working Paper 53. London: Evans/Methuen Educational   *33, 54, 66, 88, 124*

Schools Council (1977) *Examinations*. London: Schools Council   *63*

SCRE (1976) *Wastage on National Certificate Courses*. Edinburgh: Scottish Council for Research in Education   *37*

SCRE (1977) *Pupils in Profile*. London: Hodder & Stoughton   *66, 69, 126*

Scottish Education Department (1977) *Assessment for All. The Report of the Secretary of State's Committee on Assessment and Certification* (The Dunning Report). Edinburgh: HMSO   *18, 74, 97, 124*

Secondary Schools Examination Council (1943) *Curriculum and Examinations in Secondary Schools* (The Norwood Report). London: HMSO   *38, 45, 89*

Secondary Schools Examination Council (1947) *Examinations in Secondary Schools* (The Holmes Report). London: HMSO   *33, 38*

Secondary Schools Examination Council (1960) *Secondary School Examinations other than the GCE* (The Beloe Report). London: HMSO   *30, 33, 41*

Secretary of State (1977) *A New Partnership of Our Schools* (The Taylor Report). London: HMSO   *81*

Sharp, R. and Green, A. (1975) *Education and Social Control*. London: Routledge & Kegan Paul   *102, 109, 110*

Sherwood, P. (1978) The testing invasion. *Forum*, *20*, no 3 Summer   *77*

Silberman, M.L. (1969) Behavioural expression of teachers' attitudes towards elementary school students. *Journal of*

Educational Psychology 60, no 5: 402-7   *109*

Simon, B. (1953) *Intelligence Testing and the Comprehensive School*. London: Lawrence & Wishart   *47*

Stansbury, D. (1979) The record of personal experience, qualities and qualifications. In E. Adams and T. Burgess (eds) *Outcomes of Education*. London: Macmillan   *130*

Stephenson, J. (1979) The use of statements at N.E. London Polytechnic. In E. Adams and T. Burgess (eds) *Outcomes of Education*, London: Macmillan   *130*

Stones, E. (1975) Black light on exams. *British Journal of Teacher Education 1*, no 3, October 1975: 299-303   *88*

Tawney, R.H. (1951) *Equality*. London: George Allen & Unwin   *41, 49*

Thompson, P. (1974) *Assessment for Australian Capital Territory Secondary Schools*. Australian Council for Educational Research   *67*

Timpane, M. (1976) *Whither Accountability?* Unpublished paper, University of Virginia, UCEA Seminar   *77*

Turner, R. (1960) Sponsored and contest mobility and the school system. *American Sociological Review 25*, October: 855-67   *59, 62, 67, 123*

Tyler, W. (1977) *The Sociology of Educational Inequality*. London: Methuen   *94*

US Bureau of Census (1973) *Statistical Abstract of U.S. 1973*. Washington DC: US Government Printing Office   *47*

Vernon, P. (1957) *Secondary School Selection*. London: Methuen   *47*

Watts, J. (1978) Clearing the air. *Forum*, *20* no 3 Summer 1978   *78*

Westergaard, J. and Resler, H. (1975) *Class in a Capitalist Society*. London: Heinemann   *49*

Whelan, R. (1978) Universities look for solutions to falling entrant standards. *Times Educational Supplement*, 29.9.78   *127*

Williams, G. (1960) The concept of egomania in the thought of

145

Antonio Gramsci: Some notes of interpretation: *Journal of the History of Ideas* 21

Williams, I.C. and Boreham, W.I. (1972) *The Predictive Value of CSE Grades for Further Education*. London: Evans/Methuen Educational 37

Williams, P. (1974) The growth and scope of the school psychological service. In M. Chazan, T. Moore, P. Williams and J. Wright. *The Practice of Educational Psychology*. London: Longman 44

Williams, R. (1976) Base and superstructure in Marxist cultural theory. In R. Dale *et al.* (eds) *Schooling and Capitalism*. London: Routledge & Kegan Paul 99

Williams, R. (1977) French connection. Review article, *New Society*, 5.5.77 43, 75, 85, 100

Willis, P. (1976) The class significance of school counter-culture. In M. Hammersley and P. Woods (eds) *op. cit.* 115, 116

Willis, P. (1977) *Learning to Labour*. Farnborough: Saxon 69, 114, 115, 130

Wood, R. and Napthali, I.W.A. (1975) Assessment in the classroom. *Educational Studies 1* no 3: 151-61 108

Woods, P. (1979) *The Divided School*. London: Routledge & Kegan Paul 113

Wright Mills, C. (1956) *The Power Elite*. New York: Oxford University Press 119

Yates, A. and Pidgeon, D.A. (1957) *Admission to Grammar Schools*. London: Newnes 47

Young, M.F.D. (ed.) (1971) *Knowledge and Control*. London: Collier Macmillan 100

Subject index